Worshipping With Dementia

Worshipping With Dementia

Meditations,
Scriptures
and Prayers
for Sufferers
and Carers

Louise Morse

MONARCH
BOOKS

Oxford, UK and Grand Rapids, Michigan, USA

First published in the UK in 2010 by Monarch Books
(a publishing imprint of Lion Hudson plc)
Wilkinson House, Jordan Hill Road, Oxford OX2 8DR, England
Tel: +44 (0)1865 302750 Fax: +44 (0)1865 302757
Email: monarch@lionhudson.com
www.lionhudson.com

ISBN 978 1 85424 931 9

Distributed by:
UK: Marston Book Services, PO Box 269, Abingdon, Oxon, OX14 4YN
USA: Kregel Publications, PO Box 2607, Grand Rapids, Michigan 49501

The text paper used in this book has been made from wood independently certified as having come from sustainable forests.

British Library Cataloguing Data
A catalogue record for this book is available from the British Library.

Printed and bound in the UK by Clays, August 2016, LH26.

Published jointly with Pilgrim Homes, 175 Tower Bridge Road, London SE1 2AL

Dedication

Some years ago a friend called Robert was learning to play the flute. Elizabeth, a professional flautist, came to stay with me and Robert brought his flute around one afternoon, hoping for some tips.

Towards the end of his impromptu lesson Elizabeth suggested they played a simple tune together. I have never heard anything like it. Robert played what sounded like "chopsticks" for Piccolo. Elizabeth listened for a minute or so then she lifted her instrument to her lips and began to play, lilting, dancing notes that were an amazing counter-point to "chopsticks", making it sound altogether wonderful. Imagine a rough, wooden stick being loosely wrapped in the finest, transparent silk; it was like that.

According to the online Free Dictionary, counterpoint is:

> The technique of combining two or more melodic lines in such a way that they establish a harmonic relationship while retaining their linear individuality.

It's exactly what God does in the lives of His people. "Your statutes have been my songs in the house of my pilgrimage," (Psalm 119:54, NKJV). In other words, God's laws have been the counterpoint to the whole of the psalmist's life.

This book is dedicated to all those on pilgrimage whose lives are lived, like mine, in God's counterpoint. Thank you for sharing some of the notes with me.

Contents

Don't desert me

As I lose an identity in the world around me,
which is so anxious to define me
by what I do and say,
rather than who I am,
I can seek an identity by simply being me,
a person created in the image of God.
My spiritual self is reflected in the divine
and given meaning as a transcendent being ...
as I travel toward the dissolution of myself,
my personality, my very "essence",
my relationship with God
needs increasing support from you,
my other in the body of Christ.
Don't abandon me at any stage,
for the Holy Spirit connects us ...
I need you to minister to me,
to sing with me, pray with me,
to be my memory for me ...
You play a vital role
in relating to the soul within me,
connecting at this eternal level.

Sing alongside me, touch me, pray with me,
reassure me of your presence,
and through you, of Christ's presence.

From the time in her late forties when she was diagnosed with dementia, former government executive Christine Bryden worked tirelessly to make the voice of people with dementia heard. When she made this appeal she was addressing an international conference in 2005. Christine has written two books, *Who Will I Be When I die?* and *Dancing with Dementia*. They are available from her website, http://www.christinebryden.com.

In an interview with a British newspaper, she said, "It really upsets me when [relatives of people with dementia] say, 'I don't visit any more because she doesn't remember my visits and doesn't know who I am.' The visit brings a good feeling even if the person can't remember why they feel good."

And I will pray the Father, and He will give you another Helper, that He may abide with you forever – the Spirit of truth, whom the world cannot receive, because it neither sees Him nor knows Him; but you know Him, for He dwells with you and will be in you.

John 14:16–17 (NKJV)

Why worshipping with dementia?

At some point in the journey of a person with dementia a relative will ask, "What's the point of my coming to visit? He doesn't recognise me anymore. He doesn't know who I am and the minute I've gone he will have forgotten my visit." A husband not recognising his wife of many years or a mother her children is one of the most painful and cruel aspects of dementia. For a spouse who has managed heroically for years, through challenging behaviour, lack of sleep and declining health, this sudden estrangement can be a tipping point. "I felt I had lost my own identity – I had lost myself, when my husband didn't recognise me," said one caregiver. Up till then she had coped well, but felt herself swamped with the feeling that there was no sense in struggling on. Within the role of a wife helping her husband she could cope, but when she became a stranger the reason for being there seemed to vanish. With the help of professionals and her family she recovered, but she realized that her husband's needs had become too complex for her to handle at home. Not everyone with dementia forgets their loved ones, but it is not uncommon. The question we naturally ask is: if the person can't remember their nearest and dearest, how can they remember God? And how can they worship Him? What's the point of this book?

In another book (*Could it Be Dementia?* Monarch 2008) I've described a conversation with a man, whom I believed to be a pastor, at a Christian conference. He told me, "I never got over what happened to my grandma... I never got over it." There was no need to tell me that she had died with dementia, and no need to explain the process or the pain. The rest of the conference seemed to disappear and we were caught up in a conversation without words, just speaking with our eyes, his deeply grieving, mine empathizing. I thought, not for the first time, how important it is to remind ourselves of what we know but can forget in times of grief and strain – that God is not some distant aspiration but actually lives in us, (John 14:17) and has said He will never leave us (Hebrews 13:5). He has promised that nothing will separate us from Him and His love; nothing, not even dementia (Romans 8:39). So I said how blessed he was to have had such a loving grandma in the first place, and (knowing that she could not have been anything other than a Lois to this Timothy) we both knew she was alright, now. I reminded him that all the time she had had dementia and perhaps couldn't communicate with anybody, the Holy Spirit was right there with her, communicating and comforting in ways we couldn't see. "You might not have been able to see your grandma any more but she was still there alright, and *He* did," I said. He nodded. He already knew this, of course, but sometimes we need to hear what we know, as affirmation, from others.

I told him of the times in our care homes when, like lightning flashes through darkness, there are fleeting moments of grace; glimpses when the person with dementia breaks through and is seen again. A pastor, who preaches regularly in our care homes, tells of an experience that radically changed his attitude towards preaching to God's elderly children. He said, "A resident had severe Alzheimer's disease. She possessed a very sweet nature and a lovely smile, but could speak only two or three words. She sat quietly in her chair, mouth open wide and with a completely vacant look. On one occasion, as I gave out my text, her mouth closed, her eyes came alive and were riveted on me the whole time I was preaching. When I concluded, the vacant look returned and her mouth immediately dropped open. Nothing was clearer to me than that the Holy Spirit had communicated the Word of God to the soul of that saint."

He saw how, just as the Holy Spirit can unlock the hearts of lifeless sinners, in the same way He can unlock the confused minds of His elderly people. We see this in the prayers that dementia sufferers sometimes unexpectedly say. One of our home managers thinks that the fact that a sufferer can offer up a meaningful prayer at exactly the right moment is one of the strongest proofs that God exists. Far from being a thoughtless repetition of things learned long ago these prayers are fresh and appropriate.

The Holy Spirit works in ways we cannot see or understand, but sometimes we do see the results. A missionary at a well known London mission told us how she regularly visited a man with severe dementia in a local hospital, but one day felt she ought to go a day earlier than her scheduled visit. He was lying in bed on the ward, eyes shut and barely acknowledging her presence, so she quietly read to him the Scriptures about salvation. Suddenly his eyes opened and he asked her, "Are you telling me that if I ask Jesus to be my Saviour, He will forgive my sins – all my sins will be forgiven?" "That's exactly what I'm saying," she said. "That's what I want to do," he replied, and he followed her in a short prayer before closing his eyes and slipping back into dementia. When she went the following week she found that he had died the night of her visit.

In his book, *The Man Who Mistook His Wife for a Hat*, neurologist Oliver Sacks describes Jimmie, a patient who had such dense amnesia that everyone involved in caring for him had an overwhelming sense of something missing, and Dr Sacks wondered if he was a completely lost soul. He put this to one of Jimmie's carers, who suggested he observe Jimmie during a service in the hospital chapel. There he saw him worshipping, "no longer at the mercy of a faulty and fallible mechanism – that of meaningless sequences and memory traces – absorbed in an act of his whole being, which carried feeling and meaning in an organic continuity and unity, a continuity and unity so seamless it could not permit any break".

God has given His people a "down-payment", a "pledge" and foretaste of heaven.

The Holy Spirit is a seal, and a kind of magnet drawing us to heaven. (Ephesians 1:13–14.) In the daily thoughts that follow, our prayer is that His Spirit will minister as He did with Jimmie and continues to do with all of us.

O Lord, you have searched me
and you know me.
You know when I sit and when I rise;
you perceive my thoughts from afar...
Where can I go from your Spirit?
Where can I flee from your presence?

Psalm 139:1–2, 7

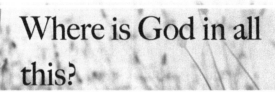

Where is God in all this?

At a conference on dementia, a man in the audience spoke for many when he asked, "Where is God in all this?" Sometimes when people ask that question, what they mean is, "How can God allow this? If God is all powerful and can do anything, why does He not prevent dementia?"

It's a question we often ask when we find ourselves caught up in intolerable circumstances. If we could take a position in space from which we could see all the questions people were asking, this one would be seen shooting constantly around the globe like a multi-coloured ribbon. Although we rarely allow God to have total control of our lives, we expect Him to take enough control to keep us from disaster. The answer lies at the very beginning of life as we know it, in the Garden of Eden, but the solution is in Christ.

At the start of human history God created Adam and Eve in His own likeness and gave them the freedom to choose. They chose to disobey God. Because of that choice, sin and sickness entered the world. Now we live in a fallen world and we are all affected by what sin produces. So in our sad world, some people suffer because of poverty and famine, some know terrible hardship due to cruel and violent conflicts, and some experience terrible diseases like cancer or dementia.

But that is not the whole story. When we receive Christ into our lives, three wonderful things happen. Our relationship to God changes and He begins to use and control our circumstances to benefit us. The Lord Jesus comes into our lives and He shows us how to live. And the Holy Spirit works in us all the time to help us in every part of our lives.

There is a beautiful episode in the life of Jesus that took place just after He rose from the dead. On that day two disciples were walking sadly along the road when the risen Jesus joined them. After some conversation He told them that the whole Bible showed that He had first to suffer and then to enter into His glory. The Apostle Paul teaches us in 2 Corinthians 4 that it is just the same for Christians. He says in verse 17 that our present sufferings (which he calls light and momentary) are "achieving for us" a phenomenal experience of eternal glory. That means that God takes the results of being in a sinful world and makes them so useful to us that in heaven we will thank God for them.

That was how the Apostle Paul dealt with the many great hardships he had to face. He said in Romans 8:18, "I consider that our present sufferings are not worth comparing with the glory that will be revealed in us."

He was walking in Jesus' footsteps. That is what we are also called to do. But what is so wonderful is that Jesus walks with us. So not only does God use the sufferings of this life that come because we are in a fallen world, but Jesus sets us the example and then walks with us and holds our hand in those sufferings. And the Holy Spirit helps us in our weaknesses. We are pilgrims on our way Home, and He is with us, every step of the way.

Prayer

Father God, thank you for your great love that overrules our sin and rebellion. Thank you that in this fallen world you use everything to make us more ready to meet you and enjoy heaven. We thank you especially that Jesus walked this earth and knew all its hardships and sufferings. May we know His comfort and strength each day. May we know the Holy Spirit within us helping us to trust you and to follow Jesus in all we do. When we feel alone and separated from you, please remind us that you have promised never to leave us, nor forsake us. Help us to take you at your word, Lord. And please bring to us those people who will encourage us, and who will bring with them your Holy Spirit. Lord, the words of the old hymn echo my prayer, and I lift them to you today:

Hymn

I know not why God's wondrous grace
To me He hath made known,
Nor why, unworthy, Christ in love
Redeemed me for His own.

Refrain:
But I know Whom I have believèd,
And am persuaded that He is able
To keep that which I've committed
Unto Him against that day.

I know not how this saving faith
To me He did impart,
Nor how believing in His Word
Wrought peace within my heart.

Refrain

I know not how the Spirit moves,
Convincing us of sin,
Revealing Jesus through the Word,
Creating faith in Him.

Refrain

I know not what of good or ill
May be reserved for me,
Of weary ways or golden days,
Before His face I see.

Refrain

I know not when my Lord may come,
At night or noonday fair,
Nor if I walk the vale with Him,
Or meet Him in the air.

Refrain

Daniel W. Whittle, 1883

Keeping it simple

Worship helps us to hold ourselves together. In one of his devotional books, Selwyn Hughes, one of Wales' best-loved preachers, pointed out that in worship we find unity, not just with God but within ourselves:

> How do we get the framework, the sense of structure we need to be able to move effectively from one day to another, in a world where everything that seemed to be nailed down is coming apart? It is to be found in our worship of God. We enter into the presence of the Lord and lo, His unity becomes our unity.

Unity – the integrity of self – is the focus of good care for people with dementia. We see in our care homes how worship contributes to their well-being, from calm when Grace is said at mealtimes, to the devotions taken daily.

For people with dementia, simplicity is paramount. Not the simplicity associated with childishness, but the elegant simplicity delivered by a good teacher. For people with dementia are not childish: throughout their lives they have learnt and experienced much. They have gone through the "fiery furnace" and the "deep waters". Even though the brain that processes thoughts and memories is damaged, the person is still the same person – he or she is an adult, not a child.

For over 200 years, Pilgrim Homes' ministry has been to care for elderly Christians. That has been its total focus, and as a result it understands their spiritual needs probably better than most. As we grow older we become frailer, and often more fearful. Old age is a time of loss; loss of loved ones, friends and family and often, Christian fellowship, and with all that we also lose a sense of trust. With frailty, life is less certain. It is not at all unusual for older people to lose a trust in their salvation, even those who have been stalwart all their Christian life.

More than ever, they need the reassurance of fellow pilgrims, and the Scriptures. Old age is a time of narrowing focus in more ways than one, which is why spiritual support is so important.

Throughout this book we've given simple daily devotions, together with a Scripture verse, a suggested prayer and a hymn. The devotions have been contributed by fellow pilgrims, including those who take services in our homes, among them Bible School graduates. They are based on the themes that we know from our experience are important to older people, including those with dementia.

Many of today's older Christians remember Scripture verses from the days when they used to memorize them in Sunday School, as a matter of course. Sometimes they like to join in reciting them as they are read out. Many people with dementia respond well to music, particularly the traditional old hymns they know so well. Until fairly recently, hymns from long ago were staples in church services, and they will never lose their glory or their meaning. If you do not have a musical accompaniment, try reading the words of the hymns aloud together. Some read like divine poetry, and have a pleasing rhythm even when read without music.

A structure to the day and a regular routine is important for people with dementia, and a good idea is to set a regular time for these devotions. Part of the routine is often a few minutes of settling down, and you may like to begin by massaging lemon balm into the person's hands, which has been shown to be calming. Begin by playing some suitable worship music – there are excellent Christian music CDs available nowadays, including some of the traditional kind.

Our prayer is that this little book may be a blessing to caregivers, too. You have an especially precious role. Jesus Himself said, "Assuredly, I say to you, inasmuch as you did it to one of the least of these My brethren, you did it to Me" (Matthew 25:40, NKJV).

Devotions

A contented mind

Not that I speak in regard to need, for I
have learned in whatever state I am to be
content.

Philippians 4:11 (NKJV)

Paul was given many spiritual gifts, such as his
ability to preach the gospel and write to the
churches. Contentment of mind and heart
was, however, something he had to learn. This
was not easy for Paul and nor is it for us. The
Lord did not remove Paul's "thorn in the flesh"
though Paul prayed for it more than once: he
had to learn to be content.

Contentment in our circumstances is hard
to learn. When things are going according to
our plan we are easily contented; once things
become difficult and trying we are swift to
complain. We ask the Lord why these things
should happen. We are often swift to speak of
our need and problems. Paul had learnt, in the

school of life, not to complain of need, rather to rest in Christ and be content in his heart and mind. There is no doubt that Paul would have found this difficult – as we do.

Being content in the Lord when we can no longer fully look after ourselves is difficult, but it is something we must strive to achieve as Paul did, because it is to our benefit.

Caring for someone who is forgetful or frail day and night is very demanding and it is really hard to be content "whatever state I am in". In these situations we need to rest on the Lord and seek to accept the situation with good grace and find in Christ a measure of contentment with our circumstances.

Prayer

> *Dear Lord, being content in the present circumstances is extremely difficult; please give strength and peace as we rest in Jesus. Amen.*

Hymn

Jesus, I am resting, resting,
In the joy of what Thou art;
I am finding out the greatness
Of Thy loving heart.
Thou hast bid me gaze upon Thee,
And Thy beauty fills my soul,
For by Thy transforming power,
Thou hast made me whole.

Refrain:
Jesus, I am resting, resting,
In the joy of what Thou art;
I am finding out the greatness
Of Thy loving heart.

O, how great Thy loving kindness,
Vaster, broader than the sea!
O, how marvelous Thy goodness,
Lavished all on me!
Yes, I rest in Thee, Belovèd,
Know what wealth of grace is Thine,
Know Thy certainty of promise,
And have made it mine.

Refrain

Simply trusting Thee, Lord Jesus,
I behold Thee as Thou art,
And Thy love, so pure, so changeless,
Satisfies my heart;
Satisfies its deepest longings,
Meets, supplies its every need,
Compasseth me round with blessings:
Thine is love indeed!

Refrain

Ever lift Thy face upon me
As I work and wait for Thee;
Resting 'neath Thy smile, Lord Jesus,
Earth's dark shadows flee.
Brightness of my Father's glory,
Sunshine of my Father's face,
Keep me ever trusting, resting,
Fill me with Thy grace.

Refrain

Jean S. Pigott, 1876

A fresh start

Now the Word of the Lord came to Jonah the second time, saying, "Arise, go to Nineveh."

Jonah 3:1–2 (NKJV)

Jonah made a terrible mistake in his life with God. Told to go to Nineveh and speak God's word, he ran off in the opposite direction and took a boat to Tarshish. A mighty storm arose and the boat was in danger of sinking. This was all because Jonah was disobeying the Lord.

Reluctantly the sailors threw Jonah overboard. Jonah must have thought as he went into the sea that he was going to die. But instead, the Lord had a great fish ready to swallow up Jonah and deposit him on dry ground.

You might wonder how the Lord could ever use Jonah again. He had made such a mess of his walk with the Lord that we might not be surprised if we had never heard any more about him.

Surely he had forfeited his prophetic office. Not so. The word of Jehovah came to Jonah a second time. How gracious and loving and forgiving is our Lord!

If you are feeling downcast because of things you have failed to do for Jesus in your lifetime, remember the Lord forgives. Because of Jesus Christ He offers His people a new start.

Prayer

Dear Lord, looking back there are many things we have failed to do, just like Jonah. Forgive us, Lord, for Jesus' sake. Let Your word come to us a "second time". Amen.

Hymn

O Love that wilt not let me go,
I rest my weary soul in thee;
I give thee back the life I owe,
That in thine ocean depths its flow
May richer, fuller be.

O light that followest all my way,
I yield my flickering torch to thee;
My heart restores its borrowed ray,
That in thy sunshine's blaze its day
May brighter, fairer be.

O Joy that seekest me through pain,
I cannot close my heart to thee;
I trace the rainbow through the rain,
And feel the promise is not vain,
That morn shall tearless be.

O Cross that liftest up my head,
I dare not ask to fly from thee;
I lay in dust life's glory dead,
And from the ground there blossoms red
Life that shall endless be.

George Matheson, 1882

A friend to strengthen

Jonathan, Saul's son, arose and went to David into the woods, and strengthened his hand in God.

1 Samuel 23:16 (NKJV)

David was in great difficulty. Chosen by the Lord to be king, he seems more like a convict in hiding than a king in waiting.

Saul, the current king, is set on David's destruction. With a large army Saul is hunting for David and his 600 supporting men. "Saul looked for him every day," reads the Scripture in verse 14.

Think what it must have been like for David, waking up each morning knowing that Saul might capture him that day. He would have wondered how the Lord could fulfil his promise and place him on the throne. Here he was, having been anointed by Samuel (1 Samuel 16:13), now in danger of being beheaded by Saul.

The woods provided a hiding place for David and his men. Then came a welcome visitor, Jonathan, who loved David and was intent on supporting him.

Saul's aim was to kill David. Jonathan, who was Saul's son, had an altogether different aim. He wanted to strengthen David's hand in God.

What a lovely meeting it must have been as Jonathan encouraged and supported David in his time of need and difficulty. Look for some opportunity to meet a godly friend who can strengthen you in your walk with the Lord today. Or perhaps you can be a Jonathan today and strengthen someone in difficulty to continue steadfast in their trust in the Lord.

Prayer

Dear Lord, You directed Jonathan to strengthen David in his hour of need. Provide a "Jonathan opportunity" today so that we may all be strengthened in the Lord's good hand. Amen.

Hymn

Here is love, vast as the ocean,
Loving kindness as the flood,
When the Prince of Life, our Ransom,
Shed for us His precious blood.
Who His love will not remember?
Who can cease to sing His praise?
He can never be forgotten,
Throughout Heav'n's eternal days.

On the mount of crucifixion,
Fountains opened deep and wide;
Through the floodgates of God's mercy
Flowed a vast and gracious tide.
Grace and love, like mighty rivers,
Poured incessant from above,
And Heav'n's peace and perfect justice
Kissed a guilty world in love.

Let me all Thy love accepting,
Love Thee, ever all my days;
Let me seek Thy kingdom only
And my life be to Thy praise;
Thou alone shalt be my glory,
Nothing in the world I see.

Thou hast cleansed and sanctified me,
Thou Thyself hast set me free.

In Thy truth Thou dost direct me
By Thy Spirit through Thy Word;
And Thy grace my need is meeting,
As I trust in Thee, my Lord.
Of Thy fullness Thou art pouring
Thy great love and power on me,
Without measure, full and boundless,
Drawing out my heart to Thee.

William Rees, translated by William Edwards, 1900

A perfect Guide

I am the Lord your God... who leads you
by the way that you should go.

Isaiah 48:17 (NKJV)

The Lord never failed to lead His people in the
Old Testament period. Sadly, they all too often
rejected His leading and wanted to go their own
way and followed after false gods. This caused
them much suffering and even led to them
being removed from the land of Canaan and
taken into exile. Yet even from the land of exile,
the Lord brought His people back and restored
them. He led them in the way that they should
go.

Ever remaining the Jehovah God, He
leads His people in the way they should go. If
you look back, you can see how the Lord has led
you faithfully all through your Christian life.

God is not going to leave you now. Perhaps
you are old and frail, forgetful sometimes and
suffering much pain and discomfort. Jehovah

your God will still lead you; He will direct you in the way you should go.

As you face this new day, Jehovah your God will lead you through each hour. He loves you as a believer in Jesus and will care for you as He leads you.

Prayer

Dear Lord, You have wonderfully led me through all the years I have been a Christian. Help me to trust You to lead me through my present difficulties. You are faithful and I trust in You. Amen.

Hymn

Guide me, O Thou great Jehovah,
   [*or* Guide me, O Thou great
   Redeemer...]
Pilgrim through this barren land.
I am weak, but Thou art mighty;

Hold me with Thy powerful hand.
Bread of Heaven, Bread of Heaven,
Feed me till I want no more;
Feed me till I want no more.

Open now the crystal fountain,
Whence the healing stream doth flow;
Let the fire and cloudy pillar
Lead me all my journey through.
Strong Deliverer, strong Deliverer,
Be Thou still my Strength and Shield;
Be Thou still my Strength and Shield.

When I tread the verge of Jordan,
Bid my anxious fears subside;
Death of deaths, and hell's destruction,
Land me safe on Canaan's side.
Songs of praises, songs of praises,
I will ever give to Thee;
I will ever give to Thee.

William Williams, 1745

A welcome Shield

Every word of God is pure; He is a shield to those who put their trust in Him.

Proverbs 30:5 (NKJV)

God's word is pure and true, every word of it. How we should value His word, meditate and depend upon it. Today we have a promise that the Lord will be a shield. This promise of divine shelter and protection has a condition. It is limited to those who put their trust in Him. Is this you? Can you say today that you trust your never-dying soul to no one but Jesus?

With your trust in Jesus, the Saviour of sinners, you have a mighty shield. Satan may say, "Look at this believer's sin!" But in Jesus we stand in triumph and hear him say, "Behold, my blood shields this soul from all sin!"

Jesus shields us constantly. His eyes are always looking out for us, watching over us. He does not sleep, He does not rest; day and night He shields His people. Rejoice today that as a believer you are watched over and shielded by the Saviour in whom you trust daily.

Prayer

> *Dear Lord, Your word is pure and true. We thank You for the word of God today and all its wonderful promises. Thank You for being our shield and for watching over us. We know we can trust You and today, in all our need, we look trustingly to You. Amen.*

Hymn

Would you be free from the burden of
    sin?
There's power in the blood, power in the
    blood;
Would you o'er evil a victory win?
There's wonderful power in the blood.

Refrain:
There is power, power, wonder working
    power
In the blood of the Lamb;
There is power, power, wonder working
    power
In the precious blood of the Lamb.

Would you be free from your passion and
    pride?
There's power in the blood, power in the
    blood;
Come for a cleansing to Calvary's tide;
There's wonderful power in the blood.

Refrain

Would you be whiter, much whiter than
    snow?
There's power in the blood, power in the
    blood;
Sin stains are lost in its life giving flow.
There's wonderful power in the blood.

Refrain

Would you do service for Jesus your
    King?
There's power in the blood, power in the
    blood;
Would you live daily His praises to sing?
There's wonderful power in the blood.

Refrain

Lewis E. Jones, 1899

Always with you

He did not take away the pillar of cloud by day, nor the pillar of fire by night, from before the people.

Exodus 13:22 (NASB)

Today, whatever your circumstances, you can be assured of the Lord's abiding presence with you.

The Children of Israel didn't ask for the pillar of cloud and fire; graciously the Lord gave this physical sign of His presence leading the people out of Egypt. He was with them continually, by day and night. They were never outside of His care, and neither are you as you trust in Christ. Look for little signs today of His abiding presence and love.

We may find the Lord's leading in our lives strange and perplexing. At times we may find ourselves in a wilderness situation, just like the Children of Israel. Be encouraged because "Jehovah went before them" (verse 21), and

He will go ahead of you today, no matter how difficult it may appear. The Lord is faithful, protecting and providing for His pilgrims in this life and in the life to come. In the Great Commission in Matthew 28:20 we read the words of Jesus: "and, behold, I am with you all the days until the end of the world."

Prayer

Dear Lord, help us to recognize Your presence and love in our lives today. We thank You for Your intimate knowledge of us and Your abiding presence with us. We ask forgiveness for our lack of faith and trust. Amen.

Hymn

I stand amazed in the presence
Of Jesus the Nazarene,
And wonder how He could love me,
A sinner, condemned, unclean.

Refrain:
O how marvellous! O how wonderful!
And my song shall ever be:
O how marvellous! O how wonderful!
Is my Saviour's love for me!

For me it was in the garden
He prayed: "Not My will, but Thine."
He had no tears for His own griefs,
But sweat drops of blood for mine.

Refrain

In pity angels beheld Him,
And came from the world of light
To comfort Him in the sorrows
He bore for my soul that night.

Refrain

He took my sins and my sorrows,
He made them His very own;
He bore the burden to Calvary,
And suffered and died alone.

Refrain

When with the ransomed in glory
His face I at last shall see,
'Twill be my joy through the ages
To sing of His love for me.

Refrain

Charles H. Gabriel, 1905

An angel's touch

Then he lay down under the tree and fell
asleep. All at once an angel touched him
and said, "Get up and eat."

1 Kings 19:5

Elijah has known great victory in his life, but
now things are different. He has run away into
the desert and now, at the end of the day, he
is exhausted and wants to die. So he lies down
under a tree and falls asleep. It seems he has
not eaten all day and there is no food readily
available in the desert. Elijah is all alone and in
great bodily need, as well as in spiritual turmoil.

An angel comes, awakens Elijah and tells
him to eat. "He looked around, and there by his
head was a cake of bread baked over hot coals,
and a jar of water. He ate and drank and then
lay down again" (1 Kings 19:6).

The Lord touches His people in many
wonderful ways. He knows their needs and
makes provision accordingly.

It may seem you are in a desert situation, but the Lord knows all about it. He will dispatch His "angels" – that kind carer, that understanding relative, that visitor from the church fellowship. Look today for heavenly provision: your Father in heaven knows all your needs.

Prayer

Dear Lord, we are ever amazed at Your heavenly provisions for us. Thank You for Your understanding of our situation. We trust You to provide for all our needs this day and we look for those "angels" to come and touch us at our point of need. Amen.

Hymn

What a Friend we have in Jesus, all our
    sins and griefs to bear!
What a privilege to carry everything to
    God in prayer!
O what peace we often forfeit, O what
    needless pain we bear,
All because we do not carry everything to
    God in prayer.

Have we trials and temptations? Is there
    trouble anywhere?
We should never be discouraged; take it
    to the Lord in prayer.
Can we find a friend so faithful who will
    all our sorrows share?
Jesus knows our every weakness; take it
    to the Lord in prayer.

Are we weak and heavy laden, cumbered
    with a load of care?
Precious Saviour, still our refuge, take it
    to the Lord in prayer.
Do your friends despise, forsake you?
    Take it to the Lord in prayer!

In His arms He'll take and shield you; you
    will find a solace there.

Blessed Saviour, Thou hast promised
    Thou wilt all our burdens bear.
May we ever, Lord, be bringing all to
    Thee in earnest prayer.
Soon in glory bright unclouded there will
    be no need for prayer.
Rapture, praise and endless worship will
    be our sweet portion there.

Joseph M. Scriven, 1855

An invitation

> On the last day, that great day of the feast,
> Jesus stood and cried out, saying, "If anyone
> thirsts, let him come to Me and drink."
>
> John 7:37 (NKJV)

Jesus came from His Father's side to this earth, and one day He gave a wonderful invitation: "If anyone thirsts, let him come to Me and drink."

Jesus was not talking about a physical thirst, but the thirst that comes from a dry soul. People who know that they have broken God's laws and commandments long to be forgiven. Without the Holy Spirit we feel that we are fine. We tell ourselves that it's a question of balance, and that our good deeds outweigh our bad deeds. But we are not measured against our own balances – we are measured against Christ. Being aware that we have broken God's laws is a sign that the Holy Spirit is at work in us, because it is He who convicts us of sin.

Jesus says simply, "Come to me and

drink." He is the answer for the dry soul. Delay no longer – no more excuses, just do as Jesus says. Take Him at His word and accept His invitation, "Come and drink."

Jesus is the answer for thirsty Christians, too. We can feel dry, spiritually, especially if our days are filled with sorrow and pain. We can be fearful of the future. Perhaps the thought of the dying process fills you with fear. Jesus knows how hard it is for us in the last days of our lives, and His invitation still stands: "Come and drink."

When we are physically thirsty, we take a glass, put it under a tap and turn the tap on. When we are spiritually thirsty, we present ourselves to Jesus, asking for His help and forgiveness.

Prayer

Dear Lord, You came from heaven to be the Saviour of sinners, to give spiritual drink to all who are thirsty. Lord, satisfy our need today. Grant salvation if we are not yet saved. Amen.

Hymn

Out of my bondage, sorrow, and night,
Jesus, I come, Jesus, I come;
Into Thy freedom, gladness, and light,
Jesus, I come to Thee;
Out of my sickness, into Thy health,
Out of my want and into Thy wealth,
Out of my sin and into Thyself,
Jesus, I come to Thee.

Out of my shameful failure and loss,
Jesus, I come, Jesus, I come;
Into the glorious gain of Thy cross,
Jesus, I come to Thee;
Out of earth's sorrows into Thy balm,
Out of life's storms and into Thy calm,
Out of distress to jubilant psalm,
Jesus, I come to Thee.

Out of unrest and arrogant pride,
Jesus, I come, Jesus, I come;
Into Thy blessèd will to abide,
Jesus, I come to Thee;
Out of myself to dwell in Thy love,
Out of despair into raptures above,

Upward for aye on wings like a dove,
Jesus, I come to Thee.

Out of the fear and dread of the tomb,
Jesus, I come, Jesus, I come;
Into the joy and light of Thy throne,
Jesus, I come to Thee;
Out of the depths of ruin untold,
Into the peace of Thy sheltering fold,
Ever Thy glorious face to behold,
Jesus, I come to Thee.

William T. Sleeper, 1887

Anger and forgiveness

And the Lord turned and looked at Peter...
So Peter went out and wept bitterly.

Luke 22:61–62 (NKJV)

Perhaps your difficulties have made you angry with someone, maybe even with the Lord.

Peter had boasted that he would never deny Jesus, but he did. Peter was self-confident, neglectful of prayer (sleeping when Jesus asked the disciples to pray) and fearful; then, not wanting to be associated with Jesus and fearing for his own safety, he followed at a distance.

We are often found relying on ourselves, not spending time in prayer and being fearful of the reactions of others. By not walking closely with our Saviour we too can deny Him. When the Lord looks at us with that look of love, we, like Peter, will be overwhelmed by deep sorrow for our disloyalty. Thank the Lord Jesus that He is always ready to forgive and restore when we come to Him in repentance.

Prayer

Dear Lord, forgive us when we have been angry and impatient. We praise You that You are a forgiving Saviour. Help us not to rely on our own strength, rather to look to You to equip us for the demands of this day. Help us to desire that close walk with You so that our testimony may be bright and bring glory to Your Name. Amen.

Hymn

Dear Lord and Father of mankind,
Forgive our foolish ways;
Reclothe us in our rightful mind,
In purer lives Thy service find,
In deeper reverence, praise.

In simple trust like theirs who heard,
Beside the Syrian sea,
The gracious calling of the Lord,
Let us, like them, without a word,
Rise up and follow Thee.

DEVOTIONS

O Sabbath rest by Galilee,
O calm of hills above,
Where Jesus knelt to share with Thee
The silence of eternity,
Interpreted by love!

With that deep hush subduing all
Our words and works that drown
The tender whisper of Thy call,
As noiseless let Thy blessing fall
As fell Thy manna down.

Drop Thy still dews of quietness,
Till all our strivings cease;
Take from our souls the strain and stress,
And let our ordered lives confess
The beauty of Thy peace.

Breathe through the heats of our desire
Thy coolness and Thy balm;
Let sense be dumb, let flesh retire;
Speak through the earthquake, wind, and
    fire,
O still, small voice of calm.

John G. Whittier, 1872

Be careful with your soul

Only give heed to yourself and keep your soul diligently, so that you do not forget the things which your eyes have seen, and they do not depart from your heart all the days of your life.

Deuteronomy 4:9 (NASB)

Moses is near the end of his life and he knows the Children of Israel will soon enter into the promised land of Canaan. In the early chapters of Deuteronomy Moses considers the past, reviews the present and looks to the future. His key message as they prepare to enter into the promised land is that they should be careful to keep their soul carefully. Paul gave the same message to the Corinthian church: "be careful that you do not fall" (1 Corinthians 10:12). And Jesus urged His disciples with these words: "What I say to you, I say to everyone: 'Watch!'" (Mark 13:37).

When we are physically weak and far from

well, there is a danger that we might forget the things our eyes have seen; forget how good the Lord has been in our lives, how faithful has been His provision. Our weakness can be Satan's opportunity to turn our eyes away from Jesus.

Moses is giving good advice: keep your soul looking unto Jesus who has gone before you. Be careful that the good things concerning Jesus and His love for you do not slip; rather, let them be in your heart all the days of your life.

Prayer

Dear Lord, let the wonderful truth that Jesus saves sinners and loves His people fill my heart today. Help me to guard my soul and remember the good things Jesus has done for me and the home He has prepared for those that love Him. Amen.

Hymn

Worship the Lord in the beauty of
holiness,
Bow down before Him, His glory
proclaim;
Gold of obedience and incense of
lowliness,
Bring and adore Him – the Lord is His
Name.

Low at His feet lay Thy burden of
carefulness,
High on His heart He will bear it for thee;
Comfort thy sorrows and answer thy
prayerfulness,
Guiding thy steps as may best for thee
be.

Fear not to enter His courts in the
slenderness
Of the poor wealth thou wouldst reckon
as thine;
Truth in its beauty, and love in its
tenderness,
These are the offerings to lay on His
shrine.

These though we bring them in
    trembling and fearfulness,
He will accept for the Name that is dear,
Mornings of joy give for evenings of
    tearfulness,
Trust for our trembling, and hope for our
    fear.

John B Monsell, 1873

Beyond understanding

Peace I leave with you, my peace I give unto you: not as the world giveth, give I unto you. Let not your heart be troubled, neither let it be afraid.

John 14:27 (KJV)

When our Lord Jesus told His disciples that He was giving them peace, He was very specific. He emphasized that it was His peace, not like the peace that most people settle for in this world.

That is why He could tell them not to let their hearts be troubled or afraid. Jesus knows about our fears and the real troubles in this world. But He can offer us a peace far greater than anything we will ever have to face.

Other parts of the Bible also tell us not to be anxious. "But in every thing by prayer and supplication with thanksgiving let your requests be made known unto God" (Philippians 4:6, KJV). Our Lord wants us to pray specifically, so that He can answer us. "And the peace of God, which passeth all understanding, shall keep your hearts and minds through Christ Jesus" (Philippians 4:7, KJV).

Prayer

Loving Heavenly Father, You know that I get troubled. But thank You that, through Jesus, You give me a peace that is greater than my fears. Please help me to remember that when I start to get anxious. Your peace is beyond my understanding. But I know that it is powerful enough to keep my heart and mind because of our mighty Lord Jesus. Amen.

Hymn

I am trusting Thee, Lord, Jesus,
Trusting only Thee;
Trusting Thee for full salvation,
Great and free.

I am trusting Thee for pardon;
At Thy feet I bow;

For Thy grace and tender mercy,
Trusting now.

I am trusting Thee for cleansing
In the crimson flood;
Trusting Thee to make me holy
By Thy blood.

I am trusting Thee to guide me;
Thou alone shalt lead;
Every day and hour supplying
All my need.

I am trusting Thee for power,
Thine can never fail;
Words which Thou Thyself shalt give me
Must prevail.

I am trusting Thee, Lord Jesus;
Never let me fall;
I am trusting Thee forever,
And for all.

Frances R. Havergal, 1874

Calling upon the Lord

The Lord is near to all who call upon Him,
To all who call upon Him in truth.

Psalm 145:18 (NKJV)

How wonderful to know that the Lord is near!
All we have to do is call to Him. He doesn't say
that we have to pray with well-chosen words.
He assures us in this Psalm that if we truly call
upon Him, He is near us.

It might be only a cry from our heart. That
may have been what it was like when our Lord
Jesus, the night before suffering on the cross,
said, "Abba, Father." Sometimes we also need
to call out, turning to our Heavenly Father for
His help.

Just as our Heavenly Father sent an angel
to strengthen our Lord Jesus in His time of
great need, He can also minister to us. Psalm
145 assures us that the Lord watches over
and keeps us because we love Him: "The Lord

preserves all who love Him" (Psalm 145:20, NKJV).

Prayer

Loving Heavenly Father, thank You that I can call upon You. Thank You for being here for me. Please let me never forget that I can always call upon You as my Father. Thank You that because our Lord Jesus died on the cross for me and rose again, I can never be separated from You. Please help me to remember how near You are every day as You keep me in Your love. Amen.

Hymn

Why should I feel discouraged, why
    should the shadows come,
Why should my heart be lonely, and long
    for heaven and home,
When Jesus is my portion? My constant
    friend is He:
His eye is on the sparrow, and I know He
    watches me;
His eye is on the sparrow, and I know He
    watches me.

Refrain:
I sing because I'm happy,
I sing because I'm free,
For His eye is on the sparrow,
And I know He watches me.

"Let not your heart be troubled," His
    tender word I hear,
And resting on His goodness, I lose my
    doubts and fears;
Though by the path He leadeth, but one
    step I may see;
His eye is on the sparrow, and I know He
    watches me;

His eye is on the sparrow, and I know He
    watches me.

Refrain

Whenever I am tempted, whenever
    clouds arise,
When songs give place to sighing, when
    hope within me dies,
I draw the closer to Him, from care He
    sets me free;
His eye is on the sparrow, and I know He
    watches me;
His eye is on the sparrow, and I know He
    watches me.

Refrain

Civilla D. Martin, 1905

Come and sing!

Oh come, let us sing unto the Lord; let us make a joyful noise to the Rock of our salvation.

Psalm 95:1 (KJV)

You may not feel like singing, but the Lord would have you sing. Sing in your heart if you cannot sing with your mouth. Sing because the Lord is the Rock of our salvation.

Our place in heaven does not rest on the work of our hands, the tears of our eyes, the church we attended. It rests only on Christ the Rock. Jesus is the foundation of our salvation. He has died for His people. He is risen from the dead and now waits to receive His people in glory. We have so much to sing about!

No one but Jesus Christ can save us. Oh what grace He gives to us that we should be His children! Every sin forgiven, every spot washed away by His blood. Nothing can separate us from His love. Eternally secure, eternally happy in Christ, let's find it in our hearts to sing to the Rock of our salvation.

Prayer

Dear Lord, help us to sing today and make a joyful noise. Although our physical circumstances may be very difficult, help us to praise You from our heart for all You have done to secure our salvation. Thank You for sending Your Son, Jesus Christ, to be the Saviour. Amen.

Hymn

Praise, my soul, the King of heaven;
To his feet thy tribute bring;
Ransomed, healed, restored, forgiven,
Evermore his praises sing:
Alleluia, alleluia!
Praise the everlasting King.

Praise him for his grace and favour
To our fathers in distress;
Praise him still the same for ever,

Slow to chide and swift to bless:
Alleluia, alleluia!
Glorious in his faithfulness.

Father-like, he tends and spares us;
Well our feeble frame he knows;
In his hand he gently bears us,
Rescues us from all our foes.
Alleluia, alleluia!
Widely yet his mercy flows.

Angels, help us to adore him;
Ye behold him face to face;
Sun and moon, bow down before him,
Dwellers all in time and space.
Alleluia, alleluia!
Praise with us the God of grace.

Henry Francis Lyte, 1834

Confidence in God

There is none holy as the Lord: for there is none beside Thee: neither is there any rock like our God.

I Samuel 2:2 (KJV)

Hannah was childless and taunted by Peninnah. They were both married to Elkanah, and Peninnah had been able to have children. Every year Hannah went up to the temple and poured out her heart to the Lord.

Set before us is a family in turmoil and crisis. Unkind things are being said and Hannah is hurting in her heart.

Families are sometimes in turmoil and crisis, often for many years. Sin spoils and separates.

The verse above is taken from Hannah's prayer in which she acknowledges the Lord's unique holiness and gives this wonderful testimony from her heart: "Neither is there any rock like our God."

In her family crisis and her own personal distress, Hannah finds the Lord to be a Rock. He is the unchangeable holy one on whom Hannah can depend. There is no one like the Lord Jehovah, declares Hannah.

Whatever your crisis situation may be, you can turn to the Lord Jesus and find He is the Rock upon whom you may depend and on whom you may rest.

Prayer

Dear Lord, in this time of crisis and need, You are our Rock. We can rest on You, for there is no one like You. Thank You for these great truths; may they be our comfort this day. Amen.

Hymn

How sweet the Name of Jesus sounds
In a believer's ear!
It soothes his sorrows, heals his wounds,
And drives away his fear.

It makes the wounded spirit whole,
And calms the troubled breast;
'Tis manna to the hungry soul,
And to the weary, rest.

Dear Name, the Rock on which I build,
My Shield and Hiding Place,
My never failing treasury, filled
With boundless stores of grace!

Jesus! my Shepherd, Husband, Friend,
O Prophet, Priest and King,
My Lord, my Life, my Way, my End,
Accept the praise I bring.

Weak is the effort of my heart,
And cold my warmest thought;
But when I see Thee as Thou art,
I'll praise Thee as I ought.

Till then I would Thy love proclaim
With every fleeting breath,
And may the music of Thy Name
Refresh my soul in death!

John Newton, 1779

Confidence in the Lord when all seems hopeless

> David said to the Philistine, "You come to me with a sword, with a spear and with a javelin. But I come to you in the name of the Lord of Hosts, the God of the armies of Israel, whom you have defied."
>
> I Samuel 17:45 (NKJV)

Goliath was an evil man determined to destroy the people of God. A mighty warrior and a very big man, no one in Israel's army felt able to go to battle against him. Daily he mocked the Lord's people. It seemed a hopeless situation.

Sometimes events in our lives make us feel hopeless too. We know it should not be like that, but it is and we feel downcast.

David went to Goliath with a stone and sling. Goliath had sword and spear and javelin. It looked like a hopeless situation. Surely David would lose his life. But things were not as they appeared to the human eye. David was approaching in the name of Jehovah of Hosts. The stone from David's sling sank into Goliath's forehead and he fell.

David had confidence in the Lord. As you think about the day ahead, it may seem that the difficulties before you are of Goliath-like proportions. Take heart and approach this day in the name of Jehovah of Hosts, as David did.

Prayer

Dear Lord, You are Jehovah of Hosts and You love Your people, never leaving them nor forsaking them. Help us to approach this day in the name of Jehovah of Hosts. Amen.

Hymn

A wonderful Saviour is Jesus my Lord,
A wonderful Saviour to me;
He hideth my soul in the cleft of the
    rock,
Where rivers of pleasure I see.

Refrain:
He hideth my soul in the cleft of the rock
That shadows a dry, thirsty land;
He hideth my life with the depths of His
    love,
And covers me there with His hand,
And covers me there with His hand.

A wonderful Saviour is Jesus my Lord,
He taketh my burden away;
He holdeth me up, and I shall not be
    moved,
He giveth me strength as my day.

Refrain

With numberless blessings each moment
    He crowns,
And filled with His fullness divine,

I sing in my rapture, oh, glory to God,
For such a Redeemer as mine!

Refrain

When clothed in His brightness,
     transported I rise
To meet Him in clouds of the sky,
His perfect salvation, His wonderful love
I'll shout with the millions on high.

Fanny Crosby, 1890

Finished!

Therefore when Jesus had received the sour wine, He said, "It is finished!" And He bowed His head and gave up His spirit.

John 19:30 (NASB)

The cry of Jesus from the cross was triumphant victory, not defeat. He had finished completely and perfectly the work His Father had given Him. That work was to secure our salvation by paying the penalty for sin. He, the perfect Lamb of God, died in our place. So as He died He was able to shout out in confident victory, for Satan was defeated and the people of God were set free from sin and condemnation. Heaven's eternal plan had been accomplished.

If you are looking to Jesus for the salvation of your soul, take encouragement from this cry of Jesus from the cross. Your sin in the sight of God is removed by Jesus' work; you are right now fully reconciled to God, at peace with your Maker. Have you done anything to contribute to this? Definitely not! Jesus has done it all – hence His cry of victory.

Our assurance of salvation must not rest on how we feel, for our feelings are changeable. Rest on the assurance that Jesus has done everything needed to secure the salvation of His people. Let His cry, "It is finished!" be the basis of your assurance.

Prayer

Dear Lord, looking at the cross, we see an awful sight, yet we hear a glorious shout of victory, "It is finished!" We praise You for all that Jesus accomplished on our behalf. Let us rest assured in our trust in Jesus. Amen.

Hymn

Man of Sorrows! what a name
For the Son of God, who came
Ruined sinners to reclaim.
Hallelujah! What a Saviour!

Bearing shame and scoffing rude,
In my place condemned He stood;
Sealed my pardon with His blood.
Hallelujah! What a Saviour!

Guilty, vile, and helpless we;
Spotless Lamb of God was He;
"Full atonement!" can it be?
Hallelujah! What a Saviour!

Lifted up was He to die;
"It is finished!" was His cry;
Now in Heav'n exalted high.
Hallelujah! What a Saviour!

When He comes, our glorious King,
All His ransomed home to bring,
Then anew His song we'll sing:
Hallelujah! What a Saviour!

Philip P. Bliss, 1875

Feeling all at sea

Now I saw a new heaven and a new earth,
for the first heaven and the first earth had
passed away. Also there was no more
sea.

Revelation 21:1 (NKJV)

Feeling all at sea is how many feel about
memory loss.

We have all seen an angry sea – great
waves and wind, a huge noise as the waves crash
against the rocks. In the Scriptures the sea is
often used as a picture of trouble in our lives
and of the fallen nature of this world. Memory
loss is indeed a cruel sea – rough, tough, and
turbulent.

As we have all seen a rough sea, so we have
also seen a calm sea, and the full beauty of a sea
shimmering in the midday sun.

As the Bible comes to its close, it makes
this wonderful promise in Revelation that there
will be no more sea. No more being tossed about,

no more suffering, no more forgetfulness. There will be a day of perfect calm, a meeting with the Lord Jesus Himself in all His glory for those who believe and trust in Him.

Carers, too, sometimes find they are all at sea, emotionally and in their caring role. Ask that the Lord would give them patience and the ability to bear the troublesome sea of today.

Prayer

Dear Lord, there is going to be a day of perfect calm when we will stand with Jesus in glory. Help us to look forward to this. And for today – let there be some calm as we trust You. Amen.

Hymn

Will your anchor hold in the storms of
   life,
When the clouds unfold their wings of
   strife?
When the strong tides lift and the cables
   strain,
Will your anchor drift, or firm remain?

Refrain

We have an anchor that keeps the soul
Steadfast and sure while the billows roll,
Fastened to the Rock which cannot move,
Grounded firm and deep in the Saviour's
   love.

It is safely moored, 'twill the storm
   withstand,
For 'tis well secured by the Saviour's
   hand;
And the cables, passed from His heart to
   mine,
Can defy that blast, thro' strength divine.

Refrain

It will surely hold in the Straits of Fear—
When the breakers have told that the
    reef is near;
Though the tempest rave and the wild
    winds blow,
Not an angry wave shall our bark
    o'erflow.

Refrain

It will firmly hold in the Floods of Death–
When the waters cold chill our latest
    breath,
On the rising tide it can never fail,
While our hopes abide within the Veil.

Refrain

When our eyes behold through the
    gath'ring night
The city of gold, our harbour bright,
We shall anchor fast by the heav'nly
    shore,
With the storms all past forevermore.

Refrain

Priscilla J. Owens 1882

God is right here with you

> Where can I go from Your Spirit? Or where
> can I flee from Your presence?
>
> **Psalm 139:7 (NKJV)**

Whatever our concerns today, we can be comforted in knowing that we worship a God who is everywhere and knows everything.

Understanding that the Lord has knowledge of all our ways might make us fearful and want to run from Him, for we know the sinfulness of our own hearts. But we thank Him that by His grace He has brought us into a saving relationship with Himself, so we have the blessing of His abiding presence with us.

In this Psalm David is comforted as he considers the Lord's gracious presence with him. And we can be comforted too as we consider the truth that we can never be outside of the Lord's presence, love and sovereign control.

We may have many trials in this life, but we rejoice that the love of Jesus is everlasting and nothing can separate us as the children of God from His presence, in this life or the life to come.

Prayer

> *Dear Lord, may our hearts be warmed by Your presence. Whatever trials we face today, help us to lean upon You, knowing that You are always by our side. Help us to look heavenward and feel Your love supporting us. Amen.*

Hymn

> I've found a Friend, O such a Friend! He
>   loved me ere I knew Him;
> He drew me with the cords of love, and
>   thus He bound me to Him;
> And round my heart still closely twine
>   those ties which naught can sever,
> For I am His, and He is mine, forever and
>   forever.
>
> I've found a Friend, O such a Friend! He
>   bled, He died to save me;

And not alone the gift of life, but His own
    Self He gave me!
Naught that I have mine own I call, I'll
    hold it for the Giver,
My heart, my strength, my life, my all are
    His, and His forever.

I've found a Friend, O such a Friend! All
    pow'r to Him is given,
To guard me on my onward course, and
    bring me safe to heaven.
The eternal glories gleam afar, to nerve
    my faint endeavour;
So now to watch, to work, to war, and
    then to rest forever.

I've found a Friend, O such a Friend! So
    kind and true and tender,
So wise a Counsellor and Guide, so
    mighty a Defender!
From Him who loves me now so well what
    power my soul can sever?
Shall life or death, shall earth or hell?
    No! I am His forever.

James G. Small, 1863

God is working out His purpose

Yet who knows whether you have come
to the kingdom for such a time as this?

Esther 4:14 (NKJV)

The Lord is in control, even though we may find
it difficult to appreciate it right now.

Although the name of God is never
mentioned in the book of Esther, it can be seen
all the way through it. It is clear that the Lord
was working out His purposes for His glory.

God was working in Esther's life; she
was raised to be Queen so she could be an
instrument for the deliverance of the Jews.
The Lord was working in Mordecai's life. He
told Esther of the plot to kill the king and the
Jewish people. And God was also at work in the
life of a heathen king, when he couldn't sleep
and was reminded of a long-overdue honour to
be paid to Mordecai.

In all these circumstances the Lord was at

work. These were perilous times, but the Lord had His plan which would be fulfilled.

The Lord is at work in our lives today. This is the Lord's time for us and He has His purposes for us. He will be faithful to us, as He was to Esther and the Jews.

Today, may we recognize the Lord at work in our lives and give Him the glory.

Prayer

Dear Lord, we thank You that You have a sovereign plan that will be fulfilled in Your time and in Your way. Give us grace to submit to Your purposes for us. Help us to see Your hand at work in our lives and glorify You for Your faithful care of us. We bless you that we are eternally secure in Christ Jesus our Lord. Amen.

Hymn

God is working his purpose out
as year succeeds to year:
God is working his purpose out,
and the time is drawing near;
nearer and nearer draws the time,
the time that shall surely be,
when the earth shall be filled
with the glory of God
as the waters cover the sea.

From utmost east to utmost west,
wherever foot hath trod,
by the mouth of many messengers
goes forth the voice of God;
"give ear to me, ye continents,
ye isles, give ear to me",
that the earth may be filled
with the glory of God
as the waters cover the sea.

What can we do to work God's work,
to prosper and increase
the brotherhood of all mankind –
the reign of the Prince of Peace?
What can we do to hasten the time –

the time that shall surely be,
when the earth shall be filled
with the glory of God
as the waters cover the sea.

All we can do is nothing worth
unless God blessed the deed;
vainly we hope for the harvest-tide
till God gives life to the seed;
yet nearer and nearer draws the time,
the time that shall surely be,
when the earth shall be filled
with the glory of God
as the waters cover the sea.

Arthur Campbell Aigner, 1894

God's provision for Noah

But Noah found grace in the eyes of the Lord.

Genesis 6:8 (KJV)

The world we live in is very similar, in a way, to the world of Noah's time. The earth was judged and all life was destroyed, except for Noah and his family. Noah not only found grace in God's sight but he also did everything God told him to do.

On dry land, in faith, he built the ark. How his neighbours must have laughed at him!

The world today laughs at Christians when we tell them that Jesus died for them and rose from the dead. They laugh when we say He is coming again!

Just as Noah went into the ark that was going to preserve him from God's judgment, we have accepted the salvation that was offered to us as a free gift from God. What a wonderful Saviour we have in God's Son, the Lord Jesus Christ.

Noah was in the ark for months, but we are saved for ever. How much better is our salvation!

Thus did Noah; according to all that God commanded him, so did he.

Genesis 6:22 (KJV)

Prayer

Our gracious God and heavenly Father, thank You for providing a way of escape for me from my sins and the judgment to come. Thank You for Your promise to me that You will bring me through all of my life's difficulties and will be with me today and every day until I am with You in Glory. Thank You for this privilege I have – to be able to pray and to be able to depend on You for my every blessing. Help me to be like Noah: to rely on You and to worship You for my every blessing. Amen.

Hymn

When we walk with the Lord in the light
of His Word,
What a glory He sheds on our way!
While we do His good will, He abides with
us still,
And with all who will trust and obey.

Refrain:
Trust and obey, for there's no other way
To be happy in Jesus, but to trust and
obey.

Not a shadow can rise, not a cloud in the
skies,
But His smile quickly drives it away;
Not a doubt or a fear, not a sigh or a tear,
Can abide while we trust and obey.

Refrain

Not a burden we bear, not a sorrow we
share,
But our toil He doth richly repay;
Not a grief or a loss, not a frown or a
cross,
But is blessed if we trust and obey.

Refrain

But we never can prove the delights of
    His love
Until all on the altar we lay;
For the favour He shows, for the joy He
    bestows,
Are for them who will trust and obey.

Refrain

Then in fellowship sweet we will sit at His
    feet,
Or we'll walk by His side in the way.
What He says we will do, where He sends
    we will go;
Never fear, only trust and obey.

Refrain

John H. Sammis, 1887

Having to give things up

> The Lord repay your work, and a full reward be given you by the Lord God of Israel, under whose wings you have come for refuge.

Ruth 2:12 (NKJV)

It may seem to you that you are having to give up things you once held dear.

In leaving her familiar surroundings, her country and her people, Ruth was giving up everything, yet she was to gain everything. It must have been a daunting prospect, starting a new life in a new country, still grieving over the death of her husband. In following Naomi, Ruth might have expected obscurity and poverty, but she was given a husband, a home, and an inheritance among the people of God.

The journey of memory loss is a leaving of the familiar, a seemingly endless trail of giving up things that once were easy. Do we sometimes feel the Lord is asking us to make too many sacrifices?

The Lord is no man's debtor. We read in Matthew 6:33, "but seek first the kingdom of God and His righteousness; and all these things shall be added to you" (NKJV).

Your present path is to take up your cross and follow Jesus; this is the ordained pathway to blessing. The believer's full reward is to look into Jesus' face and worship the Lamb for all eternity.

Prayer

Dear Lord, as today we seem to be giving up so much, help us to realize that You made the ultimate sacrifice in sending Your Son to die on our behalf. Although it is very hard, may we be willing to take up our cross and follow You. Assure us that great blessing and reward is to come. Amen.

Hymn

I have decided to follow Jesus;
I have decided to follow Jesus;
I have decided to follow Jesus;
No turning back, no turning back.

Though I may wonder, I still will follow;
Though I may wonder, I still will follow;
Though I may wonder, I still will follow;
No turning back, no turning back.

The world behind me, the cross before
    me;
The world behind me, the cross before
    me;
The world behind me, the cross before
    me;
No turning back, no turning back.

Though none go with me, still I will
    follow;
Though none go with me, still I will
    follow;
Though none go with me, still I will
    follow;
No turning back, no turning back.

Will you decide now to follow Jesus?
Will you decide now to follow Jesus?
Will you decide now to follow Jesus?
No turning back, no turning back.

Attributed to S. Sundar Singh

He does things better

... casting all your care upon Him, for He cares for you.

1 Peter 5:7 (NKJV)

Jairus was one of the rulers in the synagogue. It was a good position, and he would be used to organizing things, taking decisions and being in charge. He would be used to getting things done.

He came to Jesus because his daughter was very sick. He'd tried everything, but he hadn't succeeded in getting the doctors and specialists to help his little girl. He began to tell Jesus that He needed to come with him to lay hands on his daughter. He was so desperate that he fell at Jesus' feet. But he was interrupted in his plea as a woman in the crowd drew Jesus' attention by touching his garment. Then, as Jesus turned to listen to Jairus, someone came to tell him that his daughter had died. Jairus' heart hit rock bottom: he had done all he could to save his beloved little girl, and despite all his efforts, she had died.

But, before he had time to respond to the news, Jesus turned and said, "Don't be afraid, only believe." With that, Jairus and Jesus went to Jairus' home, where the mourners were already in full swing. It was bedlam. But Jesus went into the girl's room and, taking her hand, told her to get up. She immediately got out of bed, completely well.

What Jairus had tried to do, probably for some time, was accomplished by Jesus in less than a minute. Perhaps you've been struggling with some issues you just don't seem to be able to sort out. Perhaps, despite your best efforts, things are not working out as you had hoped.

Try asking Jesus to take over. Invite Him to be fully in charge of your life.

Prayer

Dear Lord Jesus, I often forget that You have told us to cast our cares on You, because You care for us. Before I get worn out trying to do things my way, remind me, Lord, that You do things better than I ever could. I get caught up in my struggles and need to be told, again and again. Thank You, Lord. Amen.

Hymn

Tell me the old, old story of unseen
things above,
Of Jesus and His glory, of Jesus and His
love.
Tell me the story simply, as to a little
child,
For I am weak and weary, and helpless
and defiled.

Refrain:
Tell me the old, old story, tell me the old,
old story,
Tell me the old, old story, of Jesus and His
love.

Tell me the story slowly, that I may take
it in,
That wonderful redemption, God's
remedy for sin.
Tell me the story often, for I forget so
soon;
The early dew of morning has passed
away at noon.

Refrain

Tell me the story softly, with earnest
    tones and grave;
Remember I'm the sinner whom Jesus
    came to save.
Tell me the story always, if you would
    really be,
In any time of trouble, a comforter to
    me.

Refrain

Tell me the same old story when you have
    cause to fear
That this world's empty glory is costing
    me too dear.
Yes, and when that world's glory is
    dawning on my soul,
Tell me the old, old story: "Christ Jesus
    makes thee whole."

Refrain

Arabella Katherine Hankey, 1866

Held together on the Rock

He is like a man building a house, who dug deep and laid the foundation on the rock. And when the flood rose, the stream beat vehemently against that house, and could not shake it, for it was founded on the rock.

Luke 6:47–49 (NKJV)

In the Bible Jesus is likened to a Rock. A rock is very firm and not easily moved. To put foundations into a rock is to take the strength of the rock as part of the building. When we ask Christ to come into our lives, His Holy Spirit comes to dwell in us, bringing us the strength of Christ. The foundation of our life is deep in Jesus Christ, Himself. And as a rock is just one piece, so He holds us together.

There is a contrast. We can so easily build our lives on the sand – on things that change and shift, and are simply of the moment. Sand consists of billions of tiny, separate particles and doesn't help to hold anything together, not even itself. You can only build a sandcastle when you add water, which changes the sand's consistency, but when the tide comes in the castle is easily washed away.

We are people who have built our lives on Jesus Christ. We may be buffeted by winds of change, especially when our health deteriorates. We may feel we are in the dark, as dementia clouds our light of understanding. But underneath we are held secure, because our foundations go deep into the Rock.

Prayer

Dear Lord Jesus, thank You for being the Rock of my life. Thank You that however I feel, You do not change. Please may Your Holy Spirit bring me that sense of Your presence. Thank You that when the tide of unknowing sweeps over me, I am not swept away, but held firmly by You. Amen.

Hymn

Rock of Ages, cleft for me,
Let me hide myself in Thee;
Let the water and the blood,
From Thy wounded side which flowed,
Be of sin the double cure;
Save from wrath and make me pure.

Not the labour of my hands
Can fulfil Thy law's demands;
Could my zeal no respite know,
Could my tears forever flow,
All for sin could not atone;
Thou must save, and Thou alone.

Nothing in my hand I bring,
Simply to the cross I cling;
Naked, come to Thee for dress;
Helpless, look to Thee for grace;
Foul, I to the fountain fly;
Wash me, Saviour, or I die.

While I draw this fleeting breath,
When mine eyes shall close in death,
When I soar to worlds unknown,
See Thee on Thy judgment throne,
Rock of Ages, cleft for me,
Let me hide myself in Thee.

Augustus M. Toplady, 1776

How good is our God!

The Lord is gracious and full of compassion; slow to anger, and of great mercy. The Lord is good to all; and His tender mercies are over all His works.

Psalm 145:8–9 (NKJV)

As children of God we can trace His good hand in our lives. He has been faithful in every way throughout all our days. When He saw our need He was full of compassion; when we came to Him for forgiveness He showed us great mercy; when we offended Him He was slow to anger; when we were slow to follow His leading He was patient with us.

Our hearts are full of joy and thanksgiving when we think how much the Lord loves us. We have great confidence that the Lord who has been our sufficiency in days past will be all that we need for each day to come.

Psalm 145:10 says: "All Your works shall

praise you, O Jehovah; and Your saints shall bless You." We can say "Amen!" to that.

Prayer

> *Dear Lord, as we look back over our lives, we thank you for your loving-kindness towards us. We thank you for being faithful to us when we have forsaken you. Help us today to bask in the sunshine of your eternal love and rejoice in your goodness today and every day. Amen.*

Hymn

Love divine, all loves excelling,
Joy of heaven to earth come down;
Fix in us thy humble dwelling;
All thy faithful mercies crown!
Jesus, Thou art all compassion,
Pure unbounded love Thou art;
Visit us with Thy salvation;
Enter every trembling heart.

Breathe, O breathe Thy loving Spirit,
Into every troubled breast!
Let us all in Thee inherit;
Let us find that second rest.
Take away our bent to sinning;
Alpha and Omega be;
End of faith, as its Beginning,
Set our hearts at liberty.

Come, Almighty to deliver,
Let us all Thy life receive;
Suddenly return and never,
Never more Thy temples leave.
Thee we would be always blessing,
Serve Thee as Thy hosts above,

Pray and praise Thee without ceasing,
Glory in Thy perfect love.

Finish, then, Thy new creation;
Pure and spotless let us be.
Let us see Thy great salvation
Perfectly restored in Thee;
Changed from glory into glory,
Till in heaven we take our place,
Till we cast our crowns before Thee,
Lost in wonder, love, and praise.

Charles Wesley, 1747

How much does the Lord Jesus care?

But He needed to go through Samaria.

John 4:4 (NKJV)

The earthly ministry of Jesus was demanding and busy; frequently we read that He was pressed by the crowds. Yet Jesus would make time for specific individuals in need. The woman at the well in Samaria is one of many examples of how He left the crowds to come alongside one individual in need of His help. The King James Version puts it so helpfully: "He must needs go through Samaria."

Our Saviour "must needs" come alongside you today as you look to Him. Your needs are His concern. He laid down His life for His people on the cross and day by day He cares for them. He watches over us each moment of the day. In His glorious divinity Jesus saw that the woman at the well needed Him, and so He "must needs go". He left the crowds to focus on the needs of one poor, afflicted, lonely and sorrowful individual.

The risen Saviour knows all your needs today and will come alongside you as your needs arise. His care and compassion know no end.

Prayer

> *Dear Lord, Your tender care of Your people is wonderful – we thank You for it. Help us today to know that whatever happens, You are in control, You know all about it and You will come to help and support us. Amen.*

Hymn

> Peace, perfect peace, in this dark world
>   of sin?
> The blood of Jesus whispers peace
>   within.
>
> Peace, perfect peace, by thronging duties
>   pressed?
> To do the will of Jesus, this is rest.

Peace, perfect peace, with sorrows
surging round?
On Jesus' bosom naught but calm is
found.

Peace, perfect peace, with loved ones far
away?
In Jesus' keeping we are safe, and they.

Peace, perfect peace, our future all
unknown?
Jesus we know, and he is on the throne.

Peace, perfect peace, death shadowing us
and ours?
Jesus has vanquished death and all its
powers.

It is enough: earth's struggles soon shall
cease,
and Jesus call us to heaven's perfect
peace.

Edward H. Bickersteth, 1825–1906

In the shadows

I am the Light of the world. He who follows
Me shall not walk in darkness, but have
the light of life.

John 8:12, NKJV

"Darkness" is how many people describe their
increasing memory loss.

These words of Jesus imply that the world
is naturally a dark place and needs light. Jesus
declares Himself to be that light. The Lord
Jesus can shine into the darkness of memory
loss, bringing His light into our hearts.

It is not enough to look at the light; we
must walk in it, for without that light we will
grope in doubt and uncertainty. Sometimes our
hearts are troubled and our minds in turmoil,
but we are never in total darkness, never
without hope, for Jesus, the Light of the world,
can bring us His peace.

Whilst the darkness of memory loss
can be very frightening, Jesus is taking His

children to that place of eternal light. "And the city had no need of the sun, nor of the moon, that they might shine in it, for the glory of God illuminated it, and its lamp is the Lamb" (Revelation 21:23).

Prayer

> *Dear Lord, you know we find darkness frightening. We thank you that you are the true Light, and there is no imperfection in you. May we reflect the Lord Jesus, who is the Light of the world, and lead others to know that Light in their lives. We praise you that your grace will take us to dwell in perfect light. Amen.*

Hymn

God be in my head, and in my
    understanding;
God be in mine eyes, and in my looking;
God be in my mouth, and in my
    speaking;
God be in my heart, and in my thinking;
God be at mine end, and at my
    departing.

Sarum Primer, 1538

Jesus does care

But He was in the stern, asleep on a pillow. And they awoke Him and said to Him, "Teacher, do You not care that we are perishing?"

Mark 4:38 (NKJV)

After a hard day teaching the crowds, Jesus was asleep in the boat while the disciples were battling with a substantial storm. The boat was at risk of filling with water and sinking – they were all going to die! At least, that was how they saw things. In reality, Jesus was in control and His hour had not yet come, so He could not perish.

Jesus did care. They had no need to fear. The one with them in the boat had the power and authority to still the waves and stop the wind, which was exactly what He did.

Are we thinking that our situation is out of control, that we are sinking? Does it seem to us that Jesus is a long way from us, that He is not caring for us, that in effect He is asleep?

The disciples were utterly wrong, as Jesus demonstrated to them. And, dear Christian friend, you too are utterly wrong if you think that Jesus no longer cares about you. Jesus was there in the boat with the disciples and Jesus will today be with you, and indeed every day. He never leaves His people.

Prayer

Dear Lord, forgive us that sometimes we doubt Your care, and even think that You are asleep when we need You most. Knowing that You stood and calmed the storm, may we look to You to calm our situation. Help us to trust and lean upon You. Amen.

Hymn

Be still and know that I am God,
be still and know that I am God,
be still and know that I am God.

I am the Lord that healeth thee,
I am the Lord that healeth thee,
I am the Lord that healeth thee.

In thee, O Lord, I put my trust,
In thee, O Lord, I put my trust,
In thee, O Lord, I put my trust.

Anonymous

Joy in the Father's arms

And he arose and came to his father. But when he was still a great way off, his father saw him and had compassion, and ran and fell on his neck and kissed him.

Luke 15:20 (NKJV)

The prodigal son left his father's house with his share of the inheritance and went into a far country where he wasted it all. He did many terrible and sinful things. When he was in desperate need he resolved to go back to his father in a repentant state of mind.

As the prodigal son was drawing near to his father's house, someone came running towards him, kissed him and put his arms around him. It was the father, who had seen him coming from a great distance. This reminds us that the father was waiting and looking for his son to return. What joy there was when the son was in the arms of the father!

Sometimes we stray from our Heavenly

Father. We become cross when we cannot remember things, or annoyed when we cannot do the physical tasks we once enjoyed. Yes, it can be terribly difficult to grow old. We can say quite hurtful things even to those who care for us and help us.

Our Heavenly Father is always ready to forgive us through His Son who died for us. We too can repent and find in the Heavenly Father's arms comfort and joy and peace.

Prayer

Dear Lord, draw us into Your presence, wrap Your great arms around us and remind us that in Jesus Christ we are forgiven all our sins and we can know the joy of salvation. Thank You, Lord, for Your gracious, compassionate nature. You will never give up on us. Glory! Amen.

Hymn

Jesus, I am coming home today, for
I have found there's joy in Thee alone;
From the path of sin I turn away; now
I am coming home.

Refrain
Jesus, I am coming home today,
Never, never more from Thee to stray;
Lord, I now accept Thy precious promise,
I am coming home.

Many years my heart has strayed from
    Thee, and
Now repentant to Thy throne I come;
Jesus opened up the way for me; now
I am coming home.

Refrain

O the misery my sin has caused me,
Naught but pain and sorrow I have
    known;
Now I seek Thy saving grace and mercy;
I am coming home.

Refrain

Fully trusting in Thy precious promise,
With no righteousness to call my own,
Pleading nothing but the blood of Jesus,
I am coming home.

Refrain

Now I seek the cross where Jesus died!
    For
All my sins His blood will still atone,
Flowing o'er till ev'ry stain is covered;
I am coming home.

Refrain

Wilfred H Ackley, 1910

Kept and watched over

You have granted me life and favour, and
Your care has preserved my spirit.

Job 10:12 (NKJV)

Job had more troubles in his life than most.
Many disasters struck him, including a decline
in his own health. We know from the beginning
of the book that the Lord permitted Satan to
attack Job, who is described by the Lord as a
godly man.

In the depth of his troubles Job testifies
that the Lord has given him life and favour. He
recognizes in his trials and bodily weakness that
the Lord in His providence has kept him. He is
a man who is watched over by the living Lord.

Job has lost much, yet he focuses not on
what has been taken from him but on what he
has. He has been granted life and favour, and
up to this moment Job has been preserved by
the Lord's providence. He is thankful for these
things.

We can learn much from Job about how to bear our trials. However difficult our situation may be, we are being kept by the power of God and He is watching over us.

Prayer

Dear Lord, You are watching over us and that is a great comfort. You have given life and favour and in Your providence You have kept us until now. Help us to know today that You care for us and Your caring hand is upon us. Amen.

Hymn

In heavenly love abiding, no change my
    heart shall fear.
And safe in such confiding, for nothing
    changes here.
The storm may roar without me, my
    heart may low be laid,
But God is round about me, and can I be
    dismayed?

Wherever He may guide me, no want
    shall turn me back.
My Shepherd is beside me, and nothing
    can I lack.
His wisdom ever waking, His sight is
    never dim.
He knows the way He's taking, and I will
    walk with Him.

Green pastures are before me, which yet
    I have not seen.
Bright skies will soon be over me, where
    darkest clouds have been.
My hope I cannot measure, my path to
    life is free.
My Saviour has my treasure, and He will
    walk with me.

Anna L. Waring, 1850

Looking back

> Then Samuel took a stone and set it up
> between Mizpah and Shen, and called
> its name Ebenezer, saying, "Thus far the
> Lord has helped us."
>
> I Samuel 7:12 (NKJV)

Samuel took a stone and set it up for the
people, calling it Ebenezer. It had the meaning,
"Jehovah has helped us until now."

Samuel was living in challenging days.
Ungodly enemies were often pressing hard
on the people of God. Reflecting on the past,
Samuel was able to see that the Lord had helped
His people. Indeed, He had just given them a
remarkable victory over their enemies.

When we look back over our lives, we
see many challenging days and also some very
happy days. Surely, with confidence we can say
with Samuel, "The Lord has helped us."

And, like Samuel, we live in sinful days.
Satan is ever seeking to oppress us as the

people of God, and to avoid despair we need to look back and see how the Lord has kept us and blessed us. The evidence is there, and can be seen clearly.

Confident of the Lord's help in the past, we can face the future with absolute assurance of the Lord's good hand on us.

It's good to set up an Ebenezer. Just think for a while about what Jesus has done for His people. He died to take away their sin and to make a home in heaven for each one of them. He keeps each one of us and will not let one of us fail. Believers are kept by the power of God.

Prayer

> *Dear Lord, we praise You for all the help You have given throughout our Christian lives. Help us to look back today and raise our Ebenezer. Seeing what You have done, may it give us confidence to face the future, knowing You will help us. Amen.*

Hymn

I will sing the wondrous story
Of the Christ Who died for me.
How He left His home in glory
For the cross of Calvary.

Refrain:
Yes, I'll sing the wondrous story
Of the Christ Who died for me,
Sing it with the saints in glory,
Gathered by the crystal sea.

I was lost, but Jesus found me,
Found the sheep that went astray,
Threw His loving arms around me,
Drew me back into His way.

Refrain

I was bruised, but Jesus healed me,
Faint was I from many a fall,
Sight was gone, and fears possessed me,
But He freed me from them all.

Refrain

Days of darkness still come o'er me,
Sorrow's path I often tread,
But His presence still is with me;
By His guiding hand I'm led.

Refrain

He will keep me till the river
Rolls its waters at my feet;
Then He'll bear me safely over,
Where the loved ones I shall meet.

Refrain

Francis H. Rowley, 1886

Lost everything, like Job

Oh that my words were now written! Oh that they were printed in a book!

That they were graven with an iron pen and lead in the rock for ever!

For I know that my redeemer liveth, and that he shall stand at the latter day upon the earth:

And though after my skin worms destroy this body, yet in my flesh shall I see God:

Whom I shall see for myself, and mine eyes shall behold, and not another; though my reins be consumed within me.

Job 19:23–27 (KJV)

There was Job, sitting on a refuse heap outside of town – the town where he had once been an important man, a highly respected councillor. People used to stand when he entered a room, and his opinion was valued and sought after.

Now he was sitting on a refuse heap

outside the same town. He had lost his wealth, his family, his position, and his health.

He was having a very hard time and his friends were no help at all, continually being so high and mighty and pointing out to him that it was his own fault that he was in this position. Job rightly claimed that he did not know the reason why he was suffering so much. If you read the book of Job you'll see that he was actually being tested because he was faithful, not because of any of his failings.

We all sometimes think that when we go through bad times it is because we have sinned or failed in some way. But it is because we are living in a sinful world; a world where, in the Garden of Eden at the very beginning, sin came in. Ever since then, we are told, the whole of creation has been in the "bondage of corruption" (Romans 8:20, NKJV).

But our Lord defeated sin when He died for us on the cross, and our faith in Him has saved us from the penalty of sin. We all still sin from time to time, but our Lord will forgive us our every sin because we are under grace, not law.

Isn't it wonderful that by God's grace we have been saved, and in our lives His grace will always keep us, and afterwards we will spend eternity with Him. Neither the sin of this world, nor any illness we have, nor anything else will separate us from Him. Like Job, we know that our Redeemer lives. Our Redeemer is in heaven at God the Father's right hand.

Prayer

Father God, we are so grateful to You for giving us Your Son, Jesus Christ, at Calvary. We know that we struggle in a world that has fallen into sin, but we are not condemned. Thank You that Jesus took on Himself the penalty of our sin, and by accepting His sacrifice, we are free from it. Thank You that we can say with Job that we know our Redeemer lives. Father, help us to keep our eyes on Him, and to remember that, like Job, we will see an end to sin and suffering. Amen.

Hymn

Praise Him! Praise Him! Jesus, our
blessèd Redeemer!
Sing, O Earth, His wonderful love
proclaim!
Hail Him! hail Him! highest archangels
in glory;
Strength and honour give to His holy
Name!
Like a shepherd, Jesus will guard His
children,
In His arms He carries them all day long:

Refrain:
Praise Him! Praise Him!
Tell of His excellent greatness.
Praise Him! Praise Him!
Ever in joyful song!

Praise Him! Praise Him! Jesus, our
blessèd Redeemer!
For our sins He suffered, and bled, and
died.
He our Rock, our hope of eternal
salvation,
Hail Him! hail Him! Jesus the Crucified.

Sound His praises! Jesus who bore our
    sorrows,
Love unbounded, wonderful, deep and
    strong.

Refrain

Praise Him! Praise Him! Jesus, our
    blessèd Redeemer!
Heav'nly portals loud with hosannas ring!
Jesus, Saviour, reigneth forever and ever.
Crown Him! Crown Him! Prophet, and
    Priest, and King!
Christ is coming! over the world
    victorious,
Pow'r and glory unto the Lord belong.

Refrain

Fanny Crosby, 1869

Making our steps firm

He also brought me up out of a horrible
pit, out of the miry clay, and set my feet
upon a rock, and established my steps.

Psalm 40:2 (NKJV)

One of the difficulties of growing old is that
it becomes difficult to walk without using an
aid. This can be a great trial for Christians who
once walked many miles.

However, our soul does not grow old and
feeble with the passing of the years. When He
saves us from our sins, Christ lifts the believer
from a horrible pit and sticky clay.

He then places the believer on a solid
rock, which is Christ Himself. And He gives
this wonderful promise, that the believer will
have sureness in his or her steps. Of course,
the psalmist is not talking about physical steps,
which become weaker as we grow old; he is
referring to our spiritual walk with the Lord.

The sureness of our spiritual steps is the

promise of the Lord that He will never leave us or forsake us, and the assurance that He will lead us through all our days and bring us to be with Him in glory. Christ will make sure we do not stumble or fall. In Christ we take firm steps. Even when dementia appears to take away much of our physical abilities, our soul takes firm steps with the Lord, for we walk on the Rock of Christ Himself.

Prayer

Dear Lord, it is terribly difficult to be physically weak and not able to do the everyday things we once enjoyed. Please give us patience to bear the trials. When our mind is weak and forgetful, help us to rest in Jesus and to know we are walking on a firm Rock. Remind us that we are taking firm steps to glory day by day through Your wonderful grace. Amen.

Hymn

How good is the God we adore,
Our faithful unchangeable Friend!
His love is as great as His power,
And knows neither measure nor end!

'Tis Jesus the First and the Last,
Whose Spirit shall Guide us safe home,
We'll praise Him for all that is past,
And trust Him for all that's to come.

Joseph Hart, 1759

No failure

Not a word failed of any good thing which
the Lord had spoken to the house of Israel.
All came to pass.

Joshua 21:45 (NKJV)

Everything the Lord promised happened. He
said that the Children of Israel would come
into the promised land, and that is exactly
what happened. The Lord never fails; all He says
comes to pass.

Sometimes as they wandered in the
wilderness it seemed to the people that they
would never come into the promised land. It
seemed the Lord was delaying. But now they
had arrived.

The Lord promised to give the Children of
Israel rest in Canaan, and now they had that rest
to enjoy. Rest from the fatigue and weariness of
their travel through the wilderness, rest from
the battles in Canaan, and rest from the insults
of their enemies.

It can sometimes seem to us that the Lord is slow to act. We can feel alone, even afraid, and we doubt the Lord's tender care. "How long must I be like this?" we may well cry.

Today refocus on what the Lord has done in providing salvation in Jesus Christ. Think again about the wonderful promised land of heaven that awaits His children. And recall that not a word of promise from our powerful, loving Saviour will ever fail. All He has promised will come to pass. The Lord's promises never fail.

Prayer

Dear Lord, we marvel that You brought the Children of Israel through the wilderness and into the promised land, just as You said. Help me today to see that Your promises never fail and to be encouraged to press on, trusting You for daily strength and guidance. Amen.

Hymn

Saints in glory, we together
Know the song that ceases never;
Song of songs Thou art, O Savior;
All that endless day.

Come, ye angels, round us gather,
While to Jesus we draw nearer;
In His throne He'll seat for ever
Those for Whom He died.

Underneath His throne a river,
Clear as crystal, flows for ever,
Like His fullness, failing never:
Hail, enthronèd Lamb!

Oh, the unsearchable Redeemer!
Shoreless ocean, sounded never!
Yesterday, today, for ever,
Jesus Christ, the same.

Nehemiah Adams, 1864

No fear of the future

> Then as he lay and slept under a broom tree, suddenly an angel touched him, and said to him, "Arise and eat."
>
> I Kings 19:5 (NKJV)

Fear of the future can cause us to panic.

Elijah had known great blessing on Mount Carmel, triumphing over his enemies, as the Lord had clearly shown Himself to be the one true God. Now Elijah received a message from Queen Jezebel saying that he would be killed imminently. Elijah knew the fear of facing an uncertain future.

The Lord did not direct Elijah to go away, but he went out of fear. It is so like us. We are so often impatient, and instead of waiting for the Lord's leading, take things into our own hands.

The Lord had a gracious remedy for Elijah, as He has when we are gripped by fear. The remedy was tailor-made for Elijah's situation. The Lord gave him sleep and Elijah was refreshed. He gave him food and Elijah was strengthened.

Thus it was that the Lord came alongside Elijah when he felt threatened, anxious and alone. Focus on the promise of God's word to us: "My grace is sufficient for you, for my power is made perfect in weakness" (2 Corinthians 12:9).

Prayer

Dear Lord, when we are afraid help us to look to you for peace. When we are lost help us to look to you for guidance. Help us to focus on the promises of your word and trust you today and in all our circumstances. Help us to look today for your tender helping hand. Amen.

Hymn

Saved to the uttermost: I am the Lord's;
Jesus my Saviour salvation affords;
Gives me His Spirit, a witness within,
Whispering of pardon, and saving from
    sin.

Refrain

Saved, saved, saved to the uttermost;
Saved, saved by power divine;
Saved, saved, saved to the uttermost:
Jesus the Saviour is mine!

Saved to the uttermost: Jesus is near;
Keeping me safely, He casteth out fear;
Trusting His promises, now I am blest;
Leaning upon Him, how sweet is my rest.

Refrain

Saved to the uttermost: this I can say,
"Once all was darkness, but now it is day;
Beautiful visions of glory I see,
Jesus in brightness revealed unto me."

Refrain

Saved to the uttermost; cheerfully sing
Loud hallelujahs to Jesus my King;
Ransomed and pardoned, redeemed by
    His blood,
Cleansed from unrighteousness; glory to
    God!

Refrain

William J Kirkpatrick 1875

Precious gift of salvation

Blessed be the God and Father of our Lord Jesus Christ, who according to his abundant mercy has begotten us again to a living hope...

1 Peter 1:3 (NKJV)

There are three marvellous thoughts here.

The first is that God the Father gave His dearly loved Son to be our Saviour. If Jesus is our Saviour, that means we have a heavenly Father who loves and cares for us through all our lives here on earth. Paul tells us in Romans 8 that we have been adopted into the family of God and we can cry out, "*Abba*, Father!" *Abba* is a intimate word for "Father". What a glorious relationship!

The second is that God the Father has given us the gift of eternal life in His dear Son. This gift has been given solely due to His mercy. Again, Paul said, to another group of believers in Ephesus, that God "is rich in mercy". Your salvation is by the mercy of a loving God.

The third is that we experience the joy of this gift through being "born again". The life of God from heaven has been implanted into our hearts by the Holy Spirit. So Father, Son and Holy Spirit are all involved in our salvation because the three Persons are one God, the Author of our salvation.

Prayer

> *Dear Father God, thank You for giving Jesus to be my Saviour. Thank You, Lord, for the hope that I have in Glory because of Jesus. I am so grateful that You have made me part of Your family. Even when I was turned away from You, Lord, You did not turn away from me. Hallelujah! Amen.*

Hymn

There shall be showers of blessing:
This is the promise of love;
There shall be seasons refreshing,
Sent from the Saviour above.

Refrain:
Showers of blessing,
Showers of blessing we need:
Mercy drops round us are falling,
But for the showers we plead.

There shall be showers of blessing,
Precious reviving again;
Over the hills and the valleys,
Sound of abundance of rain.

Refrain

There shall be showers of blessing;
Send them upon us, O Lord;
Grant to us now a refreshing,
Come, and now honour Thy Word.

Refrain

There shall be showers of blessing:
Oh, that today they might fall,

Now as to God we're confessing,
Now as on Jesus we call!

Refrain

There shall be showers of blessing,
If we but trust and obey;
There shall be seasons refreshing,
If we let God have His way.

Refrain

Daniel W. Whittle, 1883

Rejoicing in Jesus

There is therefore now no condemnation
to those who are in Christ Jesus.

Romans 8:1 (NKJV)

In Romans chapter 8 the Apostle Paul
reaches a wonderful conclusion: there is no
condemnation for those who are "in Christ
Jesus". The Christian will never be condemned
by God because Jesus Christ has stood in our
place and has taken the condemnation for us.
In Jesus we are free from the grip of sin, free
from eternal damnation.

Satan may often whisper doubt into our
hearts. Are we really saved? What about all
those things we have done wrong as Christians,
not to mention the many things we should have
done and did not do? Are we not all guilty, and
if guilty, then condemned?

No, those who are in Christ Jesus are
never, never to be condemned. All our sin is

forgiven by Jesus. Every wrong thing is covered by His blood.

So, let us rejoice in Jesus! Let us enjoy being Christians and knowing that there really is no condemnation to face, because we are, by grace, held firmly in the grip of Christ Jesus our Lord and Saviour.

Prayer

Dear Lord, we marvel at this wonderful statement in Your word that there will be no condemnation for those who are in Christ Jesus. This brings us great comfort and assurance. We praise You for setting us free from condemnation by the precious blood of Jesus and we thank You that Jesus is alive for ever more. Amen.

Hymn

Safe in the arms of Jesus, safe on His
    gentle breast,
There by His love o'ershaded, sweetly my
    soul shall rest.
Hark! 'tis the voice of angels, borne in a
    song to me.
Over the fields of glory, over the jasper
    sea.

Refrain
Safe in the arms of Jesus, safe on His
    gentle breast
There by His love o'ershaded, sweetly my
    soul shall rest.

Safe in the arms of Jesus, safe from
    corroding care,
Safe from the world's temptations, sin
    cannot harm me there.
Free from the blight of sorrow, free from
    my doubts and fears;
Only a few more trials, only a few more
    tears!

Refrain

Jesus, my heart's dear Refuge, Jesus has
    died for me;
Firm on the Rock of Ages, ever my trust
    shall be.
Here let me wait with patience, wait till
    the night is over;
Wait till I see the morning break on the
    golden shore.

Refrain

Fanny Crosby, 1868

Safe in God's hand

"I give them eternal life, and they shall never perish; no one can snatch them out of my hand."

John 10:28

Do this now – take a small item, such as a ring or a brooch or an earring, and then tightly close your hand over it. Look at that closed hand, then open it for a moment, and tightly close it again. The ring (brooch, earring) is safe in your hand. It would not be easy to get it out of your closed fist!

The Bible says that God holds us in the palm of His hand. No one is as strong or as powerful as God, and no one can take us out of His hand. No one can take *you* out of His hand. He will hold you fast for ever and ever. This is Jesus' promise, and He never breaks His promises.

Prayer

Thank You so much, dear Lord, that nothing can take me out of Your hand. Thank You that You are taking care of me all the time, looking after me, and one day You will take me to be with Jesus our Saviour in heaven. That is Your promise. Amen.

Hymn

My hope is built on nothing less
Than Jesus' blood and righteousness.
I dare not trust the sweetest frame,
But wholly trust in Jesus' Name.

Refrain:
On Christ the solid Rock I stand,
All other ground is sinking sand;
All other ground is sinking sand.

When darkness seems to hide His face,
I rest on His unchanging grace.
In every high and stormy gale,
My anchor holds within the veil.

Refrain

His oath, His covenant, His blood,
Support me in the whelming flood.
When all around my soul gives way,
He then is all my Hope and Stay.

Refrain

When He shall come with trumpet sound,
Oh may I then in Him be found.
Dressed in His righteousness alone,
Faultless to stand before the throne.

Refrain

Edward Mote, c. 1834

Seated with Him in the heavenly places

> And God raised us up with Christ and seated us with him in the heavenly realms in Christ Jesus.

> **Ephesians 2:6**

As a believer in the Lord Jesus you are indeed sitting in a wonderful place. Already you are in the "heavenlies". So today you are sitting with your Saviour in a heavenly place. Meditate upon the fact that the believers in glory are happier than you, but no more secure than you are in Jesus. Your sins are all forgiven by the precious blood of Jesus. You are kept by His grace and strength day by day, and hour by hour.

Discouraged by your present position? Finding today difficult and fearful of what the day will bring? Look to the Saviour and see that it's a heavenly day. Jesus sits with you, understands your present condition, loves you greatly and longs to bless you. He loved you so much that He raised you up from spiritual death and darkness, and now every day you are seated with Him in the heavenlies.

Think today about the wonderful place in which you are sitting. And remember that where we sit as believers is all of grace. "Nothing in my hand I bring, simply to His cross I cling."

Prayer

Dear Lord Jesus, thank You for saving my soul and making me sit in heavenly places. Help me to meditate on what You have done for my soul and to be thankful, even though my present situation, from a human perspective, may look rather difficult. Amen.

Hymn

Thine be the glory, risen, conquering
Son;
Endless is the victory, thou o'er death
hast won;
Angels in bright raiment rolled the stone
away,
Kept the folded grave clothes where thy
body lay.

Refrain:
Thine be the glory, risen, conquering Son,
Endless is the victory, thou o'er death
hast won.

Lo! Jesus meets us, risen from the tomb;
Lovingly he greets us, scatters fear and
gloom;
Let the Church with gladness, hymns of
triumph sing;
For her Lord now liveth, death hath lost
its sting.

Refrain

No more we doubt thee, glorious Prince
  of life;
Life is naught without thee; aid us in our
  strife;
Make us more than conquerors, through
  thy deathless love:
Bring us safe through Jordan to thy
  home above.

Refrain

Edmond Budry, 1884

Speak about Jesus

Now the Lord spoke to Paul in the night by
a vision, "Do not be afraid, but speak, and
do not keep silent; for I am with you."

Acts 18:9–10 (NKJV)

Paul comes to Corinth and speaks to the Jews
about Jesus in the synagogue. They rejected the
gospel message and were quite harsh towards
Paul.

To encourage him, the Lord speaks in the
night by a vision, urging Paul to speak out and
not to be afraid, and gives the wonderful promise
that Jesus would be with him in this difficult
task of telling others about the gospel.

Seek some opportunity today to tell of
your Saviour and His love for sinners. Maybe,
like Paul, you will find people do not want to
listen. Yet we must continue to speak and not
be silent, knowing that Jesus is with us. We
have the task of speaking of our Saviour, but it

is for the Saviour Himself to draw sinners into His family.

We have much to speak about. Jesus has saved us from our sins by taking them to Himself on the cross. He has kept us since we were first saved and has promised us an eternal rest in heaven. His love is so vast and wonderful – surely we can speak of what He has done for us!

Prayer

Dear Lord, give us an opportunity to speak of Your love to someone today. Help us never to be ashamed of Jesus. Remind us of all that Jesus has done for us, and how He has promised to be always with us, even as He was with Paul. Amen.

Hymn

Jesu, joy of man's desiring,
Holy wisdom, love most bright;
Drawn by Thee, our souls aspiring
Soar to uncreated light.
Word of God, our flesh that fashioned,
With the fire of life impassioned,
Striving still to truth unknown,
Soaring, dying round Thy throne.

Through the way where hope is guiding,
Hark, what peaceful music rings;
Where the flock, in Thee confiding,
Drink of joy from deathless springs.
Theirs is beauty's fairest pleasure;
Theirs is wisdom's holiest treasure.
Thou dost ever lead Thine own
In the love of joys unknown.

Martin Janus, 1661

Strong shoes!

Your sandals shall be iron and bronze. As your days, so shall your strength be.

Deuteronomy 33:25 (NKJV)

The path to heaven can seem to be very long. The Lord knows exactly how long our road will be and He gives us shoes strong enough to endure the road.

Whether our days here on earth are to be many or few, the Lord will give us strength for each and every day. Sometimes we worry about how we will manage in the future; indeed, sometimes we are concerned how we will manage tomorrow. The Lord says very clearly that as our days, so shall our strength be. So we can be sure that our loving heavenly Father will give us strength for this day, and when tomorrow comes He will give us strength for that day.

The Lord is promising us that He will never fail to provide for us, never fail to keep us. So as each day comes the Lord will make our shoes fit for the demands of the day.

Carers need strong shoes. Your task, as well you know, is demanding. You, too, need to know that as each day comes with its demands, so grace, strength and patience will be given.

Prayer

Dear Lord, knowing that the path to heaven can be long and the way hard at times, we thank You for the shoes You provide. Never leaving us, You give strength for each day as it comes, and so today we can trust You to provide for us, to keep us and to help us. Amen.

Hymn

Soldiers of Christ, arise, and put your
armour on,
Strong in the strength which God
supplies through His eternal Son.
Strong in the Lord of hosts, and in His
mighty power,
Who in the strength of Jesus trusts is
more than conqueror.

Stand then in His great might, with all
His strength endued,
But take, to arm you for the fight, the
panoply of God;
That, having all things done, and all your
conflicts passed,
Ye may o'ercome through Christ alone
and stand entire at last.

To keep your armour bright, attend with
constant care,
Still walking in your Captain's sight, and
watching unto prayer.
Ready for all alarms, steadfastly set your
face,

And always exercise your arms, and use
your every grace.

From strength to strength go on, wrestle
and fight and pray,
Tread all the powers of darkness down
and win the well-fought day.
Still let the Spirit cry in all His soldiers,
"Come!"
Till Christ the Lord descends from high
and takes the conquerors home.

Charles Wesley, 1741

The best sort of prayer

In the same way, the Spirit helps us in our weakness. We do not know what we ought to pray for, but the Spirit himself intercedes for us with groans that words cannot express.

Romans 8:26

Perhaps you are someone who has always found it easy to pray. Prayer is not meant to be kept for special slots during the day, but is to be a continual dialogue with the Lord, as normal as talking with a close friend. When we gave our lives to the Lord, He did not expect to be put in a corner and addressed when we found it convenient. He wants to be at the centre of our lives and our thinking.

Not all of us are good communicators. Many find it difficult to express themselves at the best of times. We find it hard to tell others how much we appreciate them, and if we have deep requests we can find ourselves tongue-tied, not having the right words. And sometimes we don't have a clue as to what to say, anyway.

But God wants to hear from us. The Scriptures say that "God was in Christ, reconciling the world to Himself" (2 Corinthians 5:19, NKJV). And He doesn't want to wait until we are in heaven. The minute we ask Him into our lives, He gives us His Holy Spirit and we begin a relationship with Him that will last for ever.

Prayer

Dear Father God, thank You for giving me Your Holy Spirit. Thank You that He knows me better than I know myself, and He knows how to intercede for me. Thank You that He knows the deepest cry of my heart. I may not have the words to express myself, but I can confidently entrust all my needs to You, through Your Spirit. Amen.

Hymn

O for a thousand tongues to sing
My great Redeemer's praise,
The glories of my God and King,
The triumphs of His grace!

My gracious Master and my God,
Assist me to proclaim,
To spread through all the earth abroad
The honours of Thy name.

Jesus! the name that charms our fears,
That bids our sorrows cease;
'Tis music in the sinner's ears,
'Tis life, and health, and peace.

He breaks the power of cancelled sin,
He sets the prisoner free;
His blood can make the foulest clean,
His blood availed for me.

He speaks, and, listening to His voice,
New life the dead receive,
The mournful, broken hearts rejoice,
The humble poor believe.

Hear Him, ye deaf; His praise, ye dumb,
Your loosened tongues employ;
Ye blind, behold your Saviour come,
And leap, ye lame, for joy.

On this glad day the glorious Sun
Of Righteousness arose;
On my benighted soul He shone
And filled it with repose.

Sudden expired the legal strife,
'Twas then I ceased to grieve;
My second, real, living life
I then began to live.

Then with my heart I first believed,
Believed with faith divine,
Power with the Holy Ghost received
To call the Saviour mine.

I felt my Lord's atoning blood
Close to my soul applied;
Me, me He loved, the Son of God,
For me, for me He died!

I found and owned His promise true,
Ascertained of my part,
My pardon passed in heaven I knew
When written on my heart.

Charles Wesley, 1739

The Lord has a plan

God… devises means, so that His banished
ones are not expelled from Him.

2 Samuel 14:14 (NKJV)

Nothing is outside of the Lord's plan. He has
devised a plan for each one of us.

Nothing is a surprise to the sovereign and
mighty Lord God. What comfort this gives us
when we cannot see the way ahead. When all
around us we see problems and hope is like a
shattered mirror on the floor, He has devised
a plan.

Part of the Lord's plan is to bring all His
people home to heaven; not one of them will be
lost. Each will be kept, led and brought to glory
at His appointed hour.

Perhaps today you are feeling like an
outcast. If you are unable to do much for
yourself and in great bodily weakness, it is all
too easy to feel unwanted and a burden. Look
again at our text today: the outcast is not cast

out from Him. You are precious to the Saviour, He died for you, He loves you and cares for you. What is more, He has devised a plan just for you. Nothing is going to happen today that He does not know. He has a perfect plan.

Prayer

> *Dear Lord, You have a perfect plan, so help me today to rest in You. Help me to enjoy and feel Your love and to know that whatever the day holds, You are holding me and will never let me go. Amen.*

Hymn

> All the way my Saviour leads me,
> What have I to ask beside?
> Can I doubt His tender mercy,
> Who through life has been my Guide?
> Heav'nly peace, divinest comfort,
> Here by faith in Him to dwell!
> For I know, whate'er befall me,
> Jesus doeth all things well;

For I know, whate'er befall me,
Jesus doeth all things well.

All the way my Saviour leads me,
Cheers each winding path I tread,
Gives me grace for every trial,
Feeds me with the living Bread.
Though my weary steps may falter
And my soul athirst may be,
Gushing from the Rock before me,
Lo! A spring of joy I see;
Gushing from the Rock before me,
Lo! A spring of joy I see.

All the way my Saviour leads me,
Oh, the fullness of His love!
Perfect rest to me is promised
In my Father's house above.
When my spirit, clothed immortal,
Wings its flight to realms of day,
This my song through endless ages:
Jesus led me all the way;
This my song through endless ages:
Jesus led me all the way.

Frances J. Crosby, 1875

The Lord is my Shepherd

The Lord is my Shepherd; I shall not want. He maketh me to lie down in green pastures: He leadeth me beside the still waters. He restoreth my soul: He leadeth me in the paths of righteousness for His name' sake.

Psalm 23:1–3 (KJV)

Perhaps this is the most famous Psalm of them all – the one we love best. It was written by King David who, as a young man, had killed the giant Goliath with a little stone from his sling.

He became a great soldier and King of Israel, but before that he was a shepherd boy, and he knew all about looking after sheep. He knew, from his own experience, what it was like to look after sheep. He also knew, again from his own experience, how God looks after us – His sheep.

Most of us have no idea what it is like to

look after sheep. But we do know what it is like to have someone care for us.

And like David, you can say, "The Lord is *my* Shepherd," because He knows *you* and loves you and is looking after you all the time. He is *your* Shepherd.

Prayer

Thank You, dear Lord, that You are my Shepherd. The Bible says that Jesus is the Good Shepherd. I shall not want. You are watching over me all the time and caring for me. Your goodness and mercy will follow me all the days of my life and I will dwell in Your house – that is, in heaven – for ever. Amen.

Hymn

The Lord's my Shepherd, I'll not want.
He makes me down to lie
In pastures green; He leadeth me
The quiet waters by.

My soul He doth restore again;
And me to walk doth make
Within the paths of righteousness,
Even for His own Name's sake.

Yea, though I walk in death's dark vale,
Yet will I fear no ill;
For Thou art with me; and Thy rod
And staff my comfort still.

My table Thou hast furnishèd
In presence of my foes;
My head Thou dost with oil anoint,
And my cup overflows.

Goodness and mercy all my life
Shall surely follow me;
And in God's house forevermore
My dwelling place shall be.

The Scottish Psalter, 1650

The Lord will provide

Abraham called the name of that place
Jehovah Jireh.

Genesis 22:14 (KJV)

In obedience to the Lord, Abraham had taken
his son Isaac and prepared to offer him as a
sacrifice. The Lord spoke again to Abraham
just as he was about to offer up Isaac, and
told him to stop. A ram was caught up in the
bushes nearby and Abraham was able to offer
the animal in place of his son.

Abraham called the place where this
happened Jehovah Jireh, which means "the
Lord will provide". Centuries later the Lord
provided His own Son to be our sacrifice for
sin. Isaac could be spared, Jesus could not. He
had to die to take away the wrath that our sin
deserved in the sight of a holy God.

How wonderfully the Lord provided for
Abraham. And how wonderful is the Lord's
provision for us, especially of His Son Jesus.

Throughout our Christian life the Lord has provided for us, and so today, with all its uncertainty, and despite our weakness and difficulties, we can rest assured that the Lord will provide for us. "All I have needed Thy hand hath provided."

Prayer

Dear Lord, You are the God who provides. We praise You for the provision of Jesus Christ to be our Saviour. Let us today rest assured in the knowledge that You know all our needs and that You will faithfully provide, as You have done all through our Christian life. Amen.

Hymn

Our God, our help in ages past,
Our hope for years to come,
Our shelter from the stormy blast,
And our eternal home.

Under the shadow of Thy throne
Thy saints have dwelt secure;
Sufficient is Thine arm alone,
And our defence is sure.

Before the hills in order stood,
Or earth received her frame,
From everlasting Thou art God,
To endless years the same.

Thy Word commands our flesh to dust,
"Return, ye sons of men":
All nations rose from earth at first,
And turn to earth again.

A thousand ages in Thy sight
Are like an evening gone;
Short as the watch that ends the night
Before the rising sun.

Time, like an ever rolling stream,
Bears all its sons away;
They fly, forgotten, as a dream
Dies at the opening day.

Like flowery fields the nations stand
Pleased with the morning light;
The flowers beneath the mower's hand
Lie withering ere 'tis night.

Our God, our help in ages past,
Our hope for years to come,
Be Thou our guard while troubles last,
And our eternal home.

Isaac Watts, 1719

The miracle of being a child of God

> Behold what manner of love the Father has bestowed on us, that we should be called children of God.
>
> I John 3:1 (NKJV)

No works of our hands could make us into a child of God. Our tears might flow for a lifetime and it would not make us a child of God. We became Christians entirely because of God's grace: He loved us and made us His by taking our sin and placing it on Jesus, who died for us. And now the very righteousness of Jesus Christ is put to our account before the Lord.

This is a wonderful thing to do. One person might die for another as a noble act. But Jesus died for us when we were enemies of God, sinners in His holy sight. This indeed is love!

Meditate upon how much we are loved by our Father who is in heaven; and meditate, too, on the miracle that by grace we have become children of God. This means we are members of God's precious family, and we are going to be with the Lord for ever.

If you are reading this and you are not a child of God, come to Jesus today, confessing your sin and crying out to the Lord that He would have mercy upon you and bring you into His family, so you too become a child of God.

Prayer

Dear Lord, it is wonderful to be Your child and to consider how great is Your love. We praise You for making us, by grace, Your children. Remind us that You care for each of Your children and that each one is loved with an everlasting love. Amen.

Hymn

Blessèd assurance, Jesus is mine!
O what a foretaste of glory divine!
Heir of salvation, purchase of God,
born of his Spirit, washed in his blood.

Refrain:
This is my story, this is my song,
praising my Saviour all the day long;
this is my story, this is my song,
praising my Saviour all the day long.

Perfect submission, perfect delight,
visions of rapture now burst on my sight;
angels descending bring from above
echoes of mercy, whispers of love.

Refrain

Perfect submission, all is at rest;
I in my Saviour am happy and blest,
watching and waiting, looking above,
filled with his goodness, lost in his love.

Refrain

Fanny J. Crosby, 1873

Timely provisions

Then the Lord God provided a vine and
made it grow up over Jonah to give shade
for his head to ease his discomfort, and
Jonah was very happy about the vine.

Jonah 4:6

Jonah found himself sitting outside Nineveh in
the hot sun. At the time he was quite angry with
the Lord because he had failed to understand
the Lord's mercy towards repentant gentiles.
However, the Lord's love continued to be
poured out on Jonah, and a vine was made to
shoot up quickly and provide shelter for him.
This made Jonah very happy because it eased
his discomfort.

When we are growing old and have many
physical difficulties and find remembering
things hard, we can become unsettled and even
angry with the Lord. Yet, as with Jonah, the
Lord continues to pour expressions of His love
upon us.

Look today for that heavenly "vine"; that little thing that brings some joy and comfort. Be very happy about it, as Jonah was; and thank the Lord for His tender mercies and never-failing care. He does ease our discomfort, and gives us grace to bear the difficulties of older age.

Prayer

Dear Lord, You have provided for us over many years and we can truly say that all we have needed, Your hand has provided. You knew all about Jonah's discomfort and made a special provision for him. Lord, You know about our discomfort too. Please give us some relief and grace to bear the difficulties with courage in a God-honouring way. Amen.

Hymn

Amazing Grace, how sweet the sound,
That saved a wretch like me.
I once was lost but now am found,
Was blind, but now I see.

'Twas Grace that taught my heart to fear,
And Grace, my fears relieved.
How precious did that Grace appear
The hour I first believed.

Through many dangers, toils and snares
I have already come;
'Tis Grace that brought me safe thus far
and Grace will lead me home.

The Lord has promised good to me.
His word my hope secures.
He will my shield and portion be,
As long as life endures.

Yea, when this flesh and heart shall fail,
And mortal life shall cease,
I shall possess within the veil,
A life of joy and peace.

When we've been there ten thousand years,
Bright shining as the sun,
We've no less days to sing God's praise
Than when we've first begun.

John Newton, 1779

Walking with God

And Enoch walked with God, and then he was not, for God took him.

Genesis 5:24 (NKJV)

The Bible does not tell us much about Enoch's life, but it tells us everything about his relationship with his Lord: he walked with God. Notice that Enoch did not say this about himself; others saw his walk with the Lord and thus it is recorded in the Scriptures.

Then one day Enoch was no longer on the face of the earth, as the Lord took him up into heaven where he could continue his walk with the Lord.

It is a great challenge to think of how others would describe us. We should walk closely with the Lord, reading or listening to His word, spending time in prayer, and being obedient children of God.

Remember that like Enoch, one day we shall be no longer on the earth – our soul will leave the body at the Lord's appointed hour – for God will have taken us.

It is a privilege to walk with God, a walk that will never end; for those who love the Lord will be with Him for evermore.

Prayer

Dear Lord, thank You that we can walk with You and talk with You along life's narrow way. We marvel and look forward to the day when You will take us to Your home. Until that day, help us to walk faithfully and obediently so that others may be able to say of us that we "walked with the Lord". Amen.

Hymn

There's a land that is fairer than day,
And by faith we can see it afar;
For the Father waits over the way
To prepare us a dwelling place there.

Refrain:
In the sweet by and by,
We shall meet on that beautiful shore;
In the sweet by and by,
We shall meet on that beautiful shore.

We shall sing on that beautiful shore
The melodious songs of the blessed;
And our spirits shall sorrow no more,
Not a sigh for the blessing of rest.

Refrain

To our bountiful Father above,
We will offer our tribute of praise
For the glorious gift of His love
And the blessings that hallow our days.

Refrain

Sanford F. Bennett, 1868

225

We will see His face

Your face, O Lord, I will seek.

Psalm 27:8 (NASB)

What a face! One day we will see the mighty Jehovah God. Though He dwells in perfect light and must hate all sin, we are going to see His face. This is only possible because Jesus has taken all our sin away by the shedding of His blood. Healed, restored and forgiven, we are by grace going to see His face. What a day that will be!

Even now, each day we can seek Jehovah's face. We seek Him in His word, the Scriptures. We seek Him in prayer as we call upon Him. We should be ever seeking the face of Jehovah. Our mind and heart should be ever seeking to focus on Him. We demonstrate that we are seeking His face by being obedient to His commands, and by seeking to love others even as He first loved us. Those who meet us should know by our words that our heart is set on seeking the face of Jehovah.

Prayer

Dear Lord, it will be a wonderful day when we come into Your presence and see You face to face in glory. Till then, help us to seek Your face every day by being obedient to Your commands and telling others of Your love. Amen.

Hymn

O soul, are you weary and troubled?
No light in the darkness you see?
There's a light for a look at the Saviour,
And life more abundant and free!

Refrain:
Turn your eyes upon Jesus,
Look full in His wonderful face,

*And the things of earth will grow strangely
    dim,*
In the light of His glory and grace.

Through death into life everlasting
He passed, and we follow Him there;
Over us sin no more hath dominion –
For more than conquerors we are!

Refrain

His Word shall not fail you – He
    promised;
Believe Him, and all will be well:
Then go to a world that is dying,
His perfect salvation to tell!

Refrain

Helen H. Lemmel, 1922

What a wonderful creation!

In the beginning God created the heavens and the earth.

Genesis 1:1

Out of nothing God created the heavens and the earth. Even though we now live in a fallen world, following the sin of Adam and Eve, the earth still has great beauty. Each season has its special glory reflecting the great Creator God. Whatever the weather is as you read this, think of what it says about the creative and sustaining power of God.

It is beyond our feeble minds to fully contemplate the creating power of our God, but it is encouraging to know that our God is so mighty. If He can create from nothing, surely He can meet our need today. He will keep us from falling. Each moment of the day and the night He will be our support and comforter.

In the beginning God created, and in the end of time He will raise our bodies to be perfect and invite all who believe and trust in Jesus as Saviour to dwell in the new heavens and the new earth for all eternity.

Prayer

Dear Lord, give us eyes to see Your beauty and power in the creation around us. Remind us that Your power remains ever the same, and therefore You can keep and support us in our bodily weakness until we come at last into Your wonderful presence in heaven. Amen.

Hymn

Thou, whose almighty Word
Chaos and darkness heard,
And took their flight;
Hear us, we humbly pray,
And, where the Gospel's day
Sheds not its glorious ray,
Let there be light!

Thou, who didst come to bring
On Thy redeeming wing
Healing and sight,
Health to the sick in mind,
Sight to the inly blind,
O now, to all mankind,
Let there be light!

Spirit of truth and love,
Life giving, holy Dove,
Speed forth Thy flight;
Move on the water's face
Bearing the lamp of grace,
And, in earth's darkest place,
Let there be light!

Blessèd and holy Three,
Glorious Trinity,
Wisdom, love, might!
Boundless as ocean's tide,
Rolling in fullest pride,
Through the world far and wide,
Let there be light!

John Mariott, 1813

When the going seems dangerous

> Therefore take heart, men, for I believe
> God that it will be just as it was told me.

Acts 27:25 (NKJV)

Memory loss can seem to be a perilous journey.

For our text today we take the words of Paul, on his perilous journey to Rome to appear before Caesar. The ship had been caught in a gale and steps had been taken to keep it afloat. But it seemed that the storm would claim the lives of those on board. In these difficult circumstances Paul told his fellow travellers that although the ship would be destroyed, all their lives would be saved.

What was Paul's hope grounded in? The angel of the Lord had visited Paul and delivered this message of comfort. Even in a storm at sea, Paul was not outside the Lord's love and care.

When we are faced with the storms of life, do we allow our circumstances to dictate how we feel and react? Or do we trust in the promises of the Lord, knowing we have a God who can be relied upon?

In Philippians 4:19 we read: "But my God shall supply all your need according to His riches in glory by Christ Jesus" (KJV). Though there are many difficulties on life's journey, our Lord will safely bring His pilgrims to the heavenly shore.

Prayer

Dear Lord, it does sometimes seem like a perilous journey. Lord, remove our doubts and increase our faith. Help us to look back on our lives and be encouraged as we recall Your goodness, and give us faith for each day. We thank You that we can depend on You – the one who is the same yesterday, today and forever. Amen.

Hymn

When peace, like a river, attendeth my
    way,
When sorrows like sea billows roll;
Whatever my lot, Thou has taught me to
    say,
It is well, it is well, with my soul.

Refrain:
It is well, with my soul,
It is well, with my soul,
It is well, it is well, with my soul.

Though Satan should buffet, though
    trials should come,
Let this blest assurance control,
That Christ has regarded my helpless
    estate,
And hath shed His own blood for my soul.

Refrain

My sin, oh, the bliss of this glorious
  thought!
My sin, not in part but the whole,
Is nailed to the cross, and I bear it no
  more,
Praise the Lord, praise the Lord, O my
  soul!

Refrain

For me, be it Christ, be it Christ hence
  to live:
If Jordan above me shall roll,
No pang shall be mine, for in death as in
  life
Thou wilt whisper Thy peace to my soul.

Refrain

But, Lord, 'tis for Thee, for Thy coming
  we wait,
The sky, not the grave, is our goal;
Oh trump of the angel! Oh voice of the
  Lord!
Blessèd hope, blessèd rest of my soul!

Refrain

And Lord, haste the day when my faith
    shall be sight,
The clouds be rolled back as a scroll;
The trump shall resound, and the Lord
    shall descend,
Even so, it is well with my soul.

Horatio G. Spafford, 1873

When we feel we're losing it

He brought me to the banqueting house,
and his banner over me was love.

Song of Songs 2:4 (NKJV)

Perhaps you feel that your former abilities are diminishing.

We have all had invitations to various celebrations, but in order to participate we have to accept the invitation. Christ invites and encourages us to come to the "banqueting house" where we will be welcomed and receive His blessings. We have an invitation from the Rose of Sharon; the lily of the valleys; the fairest of ten thousand. How we should be humbled before Him as we recognize our unworthiness and praise Him for His gracious invitation. We bless Him that He loves us and He will keep us to the end. As the Song of Songs says, "My beloved is mine and I am His" (2:16).

In our lifetime we may have many invitations, but none can compare to this. An invitation from the King of Kings and Lord of Lords to undeserving sinners such as us! When we see Him in all His beauty, does it not thrill our souls? May we praise Him for His great love towards us!

Prayer

> *Dear Lord, although we do not have the physical strength and well-being we once enjoyed, we bless You for Your gracious invitation. We thank You that You are still calling us into Your house of love. We thank You that we love You because You first loved us. Help us to love You more and to show Your love to those around us. Amen.*

Hymn

And can it be that I should gain
An interest in the Saviour's blood?
Died He for me, who caused His pain –
For me, who Him to death pursued?
Amazing love! How can it be,

That Thou, my God, shouldst die for me?
Amazing love! How can it be,
That Thou, my God, shouldst die for me?

'Tis mystery all: th'Immortal dies:
Who can explore His strange design?
In vain the firstborn seraph tries
To sound the depths of love divine.
'Tis mercy all! Let earth adore,
Let angel minds inquire no more.
'Tis mercy all! Let earth adore;
Let angel minds inquire no more.

He left His Father's throne above
So free, so infinite His grace –
Emptied Himself of all but love,
And bled for Adam's helpless race:
'Tis mercy all, immense and free,
For O my God, it found out me!
'Tis mercy all, immense and free,
For O my God, it found out me!

Long my imprisoned spirit lay,
Fast bound in sin and nature's night;
Thine eye diffused a quickening ray –
I woke, the dungeon flamed with light;
My chains fell off, my heart was free,

I rose, went forth, and followed Thee.
My chains fell off, my heart was free,
I rose, went forth, and followed Thee.

Still the small inward voice I hear,
That whispers all my sins forgiven;
Still the atoning blood is near,
That quenched the wrath of hostile
    Heaven.
I feel the life His wounds impart;
I feel the Saviour in my heart.
I feel the life His wounds impart;
I feel the Saviour in my heart.

No condemnation now I dread;
Jesus, and all in Him, is mine;
Alive in Him, my living Head,
And clothed in righteousness divine,
Bold I approach th'eternal throne,
And claim the crown, through Christ my
    own.
Bold I approach th'eternal throne,
And claim the crown, through Christ my
    own.

Charles Wesley, 1738

Where is the Lord in memory loss?

But as for you, you meant evil against me,
but God meant it for good.

Genesis 50:20 (NKJV)

Joseph eventually came to see the Lord's hand
in all his experiences. At the time of his loss
and suffering he too found it hard to see where
the Lord was. There is no need to be too hard
on yourself for asking, "Where is the Lord in all
this?"

Joseph was the favourite son of Jacob.
His brothers hated him. They plotted his
disappearance and he was exiled to Egypt. He
was falsely accused by Potiphar's wife and put
in prison.

Joseph might have asked, "Where is the
Lord in all this?" In very difficult circumstances
the Lord enabled Joseph to be faithful and wise,
and he was elevated to a position of prominence
in the land. The Lord overruled events that, at

the time, were almost impossible to understand, so that honour and praise were given to Him.

Our life experiences mould us into the people we are. How we respond to our situations moulds our characters. Sometimes we are downright resentful of our situation, and sometimes we question the Lord's wisdom, thinking we know best. But even the worst situation in our lives does not last for ever – and neither do our lives. It is best for us if we conduct ourselves, as best we can, in a way that glorifies Him. May we be given the grace to trust the Lord's sovereignty and rely on His unfailing love.

Prayer

Dear Lord, thank You for Your faithfulness in the past. We bless You that You have been faithful when we have been faithless. Forgive our doubts and increase our faith. Help us to trust You, however difficult it seems today and in the days to come. Amen.

Hymn

Who would true valour see,
Let him come hither;
One here will constant be,
Come wind, come weather
There's no discouragement
Shall make him once relent
His first avowed intent
To be a pilgrim.

Whoso beset him round
With dismal stories
Do but themselves confound;
His strength the more is.
No lion can him fright,
He'll with a giant fight,
He will have a right
To be a pilgrim.

John Bunyan, 1684

Why?

Why is my pain perpetual, and my wound
incurable?

Jeremiah 15:18 (NKJV)

Jeremiah was honest in his prayer. He wanted
to know why he was suffering, and why it was
not getting any better. Both the person with
dementia and the caregiver(s) do feel that it is
a perpetual pain and an incurable wound.

The Lord answered Jeremiah, just as He
will surely answer your prayer today: "I am with
you to save you and to deliver you" (verse 20).

For those who believe and trust in Jesus,
the truth remains that He is with you. He will
save and deliver you. Perhaps you face some
particular challenge today and, like Jeremiah,
you do not know how to deal with it. Be assured
that the Lord is with you; ask Him to help you.
Be comforted to know you are not on your own;
Jesus is with you. The Jesus whose pain on the
cross in bearing our sin is beyond our knowing

now stands with us in each moment of the day and night to comfort, support and assure us of His love.

Jeremiah was not given an exact answer to his question, "Why?" It is more than likely that you, too, will not know the answer to your question, "Why me?" But it is enough to know that "I am with you to save you and to deliver you."

Prayer

Dear Lord, we ask You, who suffered so much for us on the cross, to be with us in our suffering today. Help us to rest in You and not to be fretful about the "Why?" Amen.

Hymn

Abide with me; fast falls the eventide;
The darkness deepens; Lord with me
    abide.
When other helpers fail and comforts
    flee,
Help of the helpless, O abide with me.

Swift to its close ebbs out life's little day;
Earth's joys grow dim; its glories pass
    away;
Change and decay in all around I see;
O Thou who changest not, abide with
    me.

Thou on my head in early youth didst
    smile;
And, though rebellious and perverse
    meanwhile,
Thou hast not left me, oft as I left Thee,
On to the close, O Lord, abide with me.

I need Thy presence every passing hour.
What but Thy grace can foil the
    tempter's power?

Who, like Thyself, my guide and stay can
be?
Through cloud and sunshine, Lord, abide
with me.

I fear no foe, with Thee at hand to bless;
Ills have no weight, and tears no
bitterness.
Where is death's sting? Where, grave, thy
victory?
I triumph still, if Thou abide with me.

Hold Thou Thy cross before my closing
eyes;
Shine through the gloom and point me
to the skies.
Heaven's morning breaks, and earth's
vain shadows flee;
In life, in death, O Lord, abide with me.

Henry F. Lyte 1847

You are not alone

And the Angel of the Lord appeared to him, and said to him, "The Lord is with you, you mighty man of valour!"

Judges 6:12

The Midianites were giving Israel a hard time. In Judges 6:6 we read: "Israel was made very poor because of the Midianites. And the sons of Israel cried to Jehovah." The Lord heard the prayer of His afflicted people and the Angel of the Lord came to Gideon. At the time Gideon was going about his normal work – he was threshing the wheat. The Bible tells us he was doing this near the winepress in order to hide the wheat from the Midianites.

In other words, Gideon was going about his daily tasks, but in fear of the enemy. Perhaps this is how you are feeling today: perhaps you are having a hard time. Your circumstances, perhaps, are making you feel poor.

Being told "Jehovah is with you" would

have been a great encouragement to Gideon. May it be an encouragement today to you, to know that none other than Jehovah is with you.

Notice that Gideon is described by the Angel of Jehovah as a "mighty warrior". There he was, hiding away as he threshed his wheat, afraid of what might happen at any moment. But in the eyes of the Lord, Gideon was a "mighty warrior". As you trust in Jesus for your salvation, you too are a 'mighty warrior' in the eyes of Jehovah God. You may not feel like it, but that is what you are!

Prayer

Dear Lord, come to us in all our weakness and fear, and remind us that in Jesus Your Son, we are mighty warriors. Help us to know that we are never alone, that You are always near us. Amen.

Hymn

Onward, Christian soldiers, marching as
to war,
With the cross of Jesus going on before.
Christ, the royal Master, leads against
the foe;
Forward into battle see His banners go!

Refrain:
*Onward, Christian soldiers, marching as
to war,*
With the cross of Jesus going on before.

At the sign of triumph Satan's host doth
flee;
On then, Christian soldiers, on to
victory!
Hell's foundations quiver at the shout of
praise;
Brothers lift your voices, loud your
anthems raise.

Refrain

Like a mighty army moves the church of
    God;
Brothers, we are treading where the
    saints have trod.
We are not divided, all one body we,
One in hope and doctrine, one in charity.

Refrain

What the saints established that I hold
    for true.
What the saints believèd, that I believe too.
Long as earth endureth, men the faith
    will hold,
Kingdoms, nations, empires, in
    destruction rolled.

Refrain

Crowns and thrones may perish,
    kingdoms rise and wane,
But the church of Jesus constant will
    remain.
Gates of hell can never 'gainst that
    church prevail;
We have Christ's own promise, and that
    cannot fail.

Refrain

Onward then, ye people, join our happy
    throng,
Blend with ours your voices in the
    triumph song.
Glory, laud and honour unto Christ the
    King,
This through countless ages men and
    angels sing.

Refrain

Sabine Baring-Gould, 1865

When you want to help, but don't know what to do

Some practical suggestions for visiting

For most of us, relating to someone with dementia is an entirely new experience. It's unlike anything we've known before, and we feel we don't know what to do, or how to respond. As a result we tend to stay away from the situation, avoiding both the person and the caregivers. But visiting them isn't exactly rocket science – it just takes prayer, empathy and willingness. "Bear one another's burdens, and thereby fulfil the law of Christ", we're told (Galatians 6:2, NASB). The first bit of advice, then, is *just do it!*

Before your visit

- Unless you already know the person very well, find out as much as you can about them before your visit. They will have a personal history, which will include deeply held beliefs and values. Some phrases will be especially meaningful and comforting to them, and can act as triggers for good or for bad! Find out from the caregiver or the carer in their nursing or care home as much information as you can about these things.

- Check whether or not the person uses a hearing aid or spectacles, and make sure they have them available and use them.

- If you are leading devotions or any spiritual activity, use the version of the Bible and the types of hymns that the people are familiar with. "How Great Thou Art" is more meaningful to older people than the more modern "How Great Is Our God", for example, and the old King James Version than more modern translations. This is very important, as older memories stay intact longer than later ones. Remember, your preferences are irrelevant! It's what they know and can relate to that matters.

- Find out how they like to be addressed. First names may well be acceptable, but let them decide, or their caregiver, who knows them best.

- Take their background into account in the way you speak and pray. Some may prefer prayers read from the Book of Common Prayer, whereas some prefer spontaneous prayer. Reading familiar prayers can be a great comfort when someone is struggling with uncertainty.

- The sense of touch is very important to some people with dementia. Check with the caregiver or the carer at the home. If the individual likes to hold hands, do so very gently, remembering the fragility of old age. Sometimes the individual likes to touch you – perhaps stroking your arm. Be sure you know in advance.

- Check your information and understanding with the caregiver, especially before your first visit. Usually they are only too pleased that you are taking the trouble to help.

During your visit

- On the way to your visit, check your own emotional baggage. People with dementia are super-sensitive to moods and feelings. Psalm 139:23–24 is a good checkpoint! If there are unresolved issues, put them behind you.

- Keep each session brief and direct, speaking clearly and not too quickly. Don't shout or raise your voice, unless the person is quite deaf.

- Sit close, if appropriate, and maintain good eye contact, and a relaxed, friendly expression. People with dementia are particularly sensitive to body language and unexpressed emotion.

- Be consistent in all you do and say. Avoid hurrying or quick changes of activity or subject.

- Do not condescend or talk "across" them. Involve them in everything you say and do.

- Never scold, humiliate or correct them. Remember, their cognitive abilities are damaged. Your visit is meant to encourage and uplift them, not create turmoil and anxiety.

- Do not feel obliged to challenge their version of reality. Research shows that as the condition progresses, memories are gradually lost, beginning with the latest. It may be that the sufferer is living in a world that is in the past – but it is not an imagined world. They are not being delusional. Their world is very real, but it belongs to the past. They cannot comprehend the present "reality" because of the brain damage.

- Look for meaning in what they say and do. Try to "look beneath". If someone is saying something irrational, perhaps even "gibberish", be respectful and try to read their body language. Always treat them with love and concern. If possible, use their "errors" as a stepping-stone for meaningful contact.

- Take everything one step at a time. Think "linear".

- Focus on their remaining abilities, and do things in small steps.

- Remember – keep it simple, keep it short and keep it sweet! Don't overload them with information or ideas.

- Don't be afraid to repeat things, but do so gently, and with patience.
- In coming to a spiritual activity, such as praying, reading from the Bible or singing a hymn, tell them clearly what you are about to do. Repeat yourself gently if they wander off onto a different subject. Tell them when you are going to sing and try to get them to join in. You will have found out in advance what hymns or songs are relevant to them. We all love our old favourites, and when you have dementia these old favourites are touchstones for happy memories and feelings.
- Speak about reassuring things. Loss of assurance and loss of confidence in God are not unusual in frailty and confusion.
- Encourage them from the Scriptures when they express guilt and fears. Make a note of Hebrews 13:5–6; 2 Timothy 2:19; Psalm 71:18; John 20:38–30; Psalm 103:13–14; and Romans 8:28–30, 34–37.
- There may be particular passages of Scripture or hymns that they will respond to more than

others – don't worry about using them again and again.

- Draw on things they will know – for example, events of their childhood, Sunday School songs, familiar hymns and well-known Bible stories. Use pictures, photographs, or things that will remind them.

- Speak frequently about Christ and the cross. Talk gently, rather than preach. Don't be aggressive! Remind them of the glories of heaven, using the Scriptures when you can – for example, John 14:1–3; Revelation 21:3–5; 22:1–4; Jude 24. There are many more you probably know well.

- It's always good to pray, briefly, at the end of your visit. Prayer brings calm and a sense of peace as the Holy Spirit ministers.

- If possible, check with the person's caregiver how they felt the visit went. Was there anything else you could be doing or saying? Or was there perhaps something that was not helpful?

The Servant Song

Brother, sister, let me serve you,
let me be as Christ to you;
pray that I may have the grace to
let you be my servant too.

We are pilgrims on a journey,
and companions on the road;
we are here to help each other
walk the mile and bear the load.

I will hold the Christ-light for you
in the night-time of your fear;
I will hold my hand out to you,
speak the peace you long to hear.

I will weep when you are weeping;
when you laugh I'll laugh with you;
I will share your joy and sorrow
till we've seen this journey through.

When we sing to God in heaven
we shall find such harmony,
born of all we've known together
of Christ's love and agony.

Brother, sister, let me serve you,
let me be as Christ to you;
pray that I may have the grace to
let you be my servant too.

Richard Gillard

(© Kingsway's Thankyou Music,

with permission of Song Solutions,

Print Licence No. PL1055)

Acknowledgments

Contributions for this book have come from a number of people. We have diverse backgrounds and experiences but share a common theme: we are all pilgrims on our way Home.

Some of us have personal experience of a family member with dementia. Some are Bible College graduates, pastors and preachers; some are teachers, and specialist nurses. In making their contributions they've drawn on their experiences and expertise, and have willingly given their precious time for this book. I'm especially grateful to Pastor Roger Hitchings, author and Pilgrim Homes' trustee; Graham Brownsell, Vice Chairman, and his wife Anne; Janet Jacob, registered mental nurse and former home manager; Joy Bulling, former teacher; Philip Grist, former pastor and missionary; and Carol Taplin, Hospital Chaplain and pastor.

Most of us are connected in some way

with Pilgrim Homes, the charity established in 1807 to care specifically for older Christians. Galatians 6:10 says: "Therefore, as we have opportunity, let us do good to all, especially to those who are of the household of faith" (NKJV). *Especially* means "above all", "chiefly", "principally", and shows God's concern for His older saints.

We've all seen for ourselves how worship is a blessing to saints with dementia. I mean "saints" in the biblical sense of the word – that is, those people who belong to God. Psalm 16:3 says: "As for the saints who are on the earth, they are the excellent ones, in whom is all my delight" (NKJV). Like us, they are all pilgrims, at different stages of their journeys. For those whose trek takes them through the shadowlands of dementia, our prayer is that this book will be a help and encouragement, and a little light on the way, illuminating the ancient landmarks and the signposts that are guiding us all Home.

Louise Morse

Contact Pilgrim Homes:

Pilgrim Homes
175 Tower Bridge Road
London
SE1 2AL
Tel: 0300 303 1400

www.pilgrimhomes.org.uk
info@pilgrimhomes.org.uk